CARPS

CARPS

THE RUGBY WORLD CUP'S FATHER

The Biography of John Kendall-Carpenter

Steve Tomlin

AMBERLEY

First published 2023

Amberley Publishing
The Hill, Stroud
Gloucestershire, GL5 4EP

www.amberley-books.com

British Library Cataloguing in Publication Data.
A catalogue record for this book is available from the British Library.

ISBN 978 1 3981 0760 1 (paperback)
ISBN 978 1 3981 0761 8 (ebook)

1 2 3 4 5 6 7 8 9 10

Typeset in 9.5pt on 12pt Sabon.
Typesetting by SJmagic DESIGN SERVICES, India.
Printed in the UK.

Contents

Foreword

John Kendall-Carpenter was one of the presidents of the Rugby Union during the time when I was leading the England team. In those days players and officials rarely – if ever – mixed except on formal occasions, and so I never got to know him well.

It is now over thirty years since his premature death but World Rugby's flagship is without doubt the World Cup and it owes him a great debt for the major part he played in getting it off the ground in the first place.

This was never going to be easy. The countries in the Southern Hemisphere, supported by France, were extremely keen to get such a competition up and going, whereas the more conservative officials in the United Kingdom and Ireland were at best lukewarm and in many cases violently opposed to the entire concept.

To somehow bridge this divide, draw in the supposedly lesser countries and deliver an initial competition took a man with great diplomacy, stamina, persistence and no little amount of courage.

World Rugby is now looking forward to its tenth World Cup competition during which time it has grown to become the third biggest international sporting event on the planet surpassed only by the FIFA World Cup and the Olympic Games.

Only older rugby fans will remember John Kendall-Carpenter as an outstanding player of his era but his contribution to the modern world game as we know it today was enormous.

This is his story.

Sir Bill Beaumont
Chairman of World Rugby
2023

Introduction

Nelson Mandela is dressed symbolically in the green and gold Springbok jersey as he steps forward to present a glittering trophy to the tall, blond South African captain Francois Pienaar. It is June 1995 and countless millions across the world look on as one of the most memorable moments in the history of world sport unfolds on television before their eyes. That moment, perhaps more than any other, symbolised not only the true birth of the Rainbow Nation in South Africa but also the arrival at long last of Rugby Union onto the global sporting stage.

Mandela's autobiography was entitled the *Long Walk to Freedom* and the sport itself had trodden a very lengthy path since the birth of the legend, recalling how William Webb Ellis had reputedly picked up and run with a football at Rugby School. This single defiant act was to give both the emerging new sport his school's name and his own to the new trophy itself, which Pienaar now held aloft to the adoring thousands packed into Johannesburg's renovated Ellis Park stadium.

Indeed, the sport of rugby itself would no longer be quite the same. Within a few short weeks the leaders of the game were to meet in Paris and finally open the door to professionalism. This came after over a century of conducting what seemed like trench warfare in the increasingly desperate efforts to maintain and indeed enforce its strict code of amateurism among all its players at every level.

One face was missing from among the vast crowd, a man who had shouldered the heavy responsibility of somehow bridging the apparently irreconcilable differences between the major rugby-playing nations. The Southern Hemisphere representatives were eager for the game to progress to a global competition in ways that football, and to a lesser extent cricket, had already achieved over the years and were becoming increasingly impatient with the apparent reluctance and foot-dragging of the so-called 'Home Unions' which constituted the four nations of the British Isles.

Furthermore, if there was ever going to be a competition of a truly 'World' nature then all the other countries who played the sport in a significant way had to be considered as well. These included not only France but also Italy, Romania,

Japan, Argentina, Fiji and Canada who could all field relatively powerful teams in their own right. France of course was already as strong, and often significantly stronger, than their British opponents and were by then operating as full members of what was then known as the International Rugby Football Board. This organisation, rather in the manner of FIFA in football, would be expected to be the ones to run any such competition were it to take place.

That missing face would have been that of John Kendall-Carpenter, a man with a highly distinguished playing record and great personal integrity who, through a succession of improbable circumstances, found himself thrust into the epicentre of a sporting political maelstrom. As with Mandela, he had also trodden a very long road – in his case from a small town in Cornwall via Oxford, England and a career in education to becoming the catalyst for making a World Cup actually happen. Of course, John never suffered anything remotely like Mandela and any attempt to press the comparison too far would be ridiculous if not impertinent, but the fact remains that it was Kendall-Carpenter's patient diplomacy a decade earlier which finally enabled Mandela's gesture to be played out before the world.

Having seen the inaugural competition launched safely in 1987, he had since died suddenly and prematurely of a heart attack in 1990 at the age of only sixty-four. To the very end he had continued to wrestle with the arrangements for a second World Cup scheduled to be held in Britain and France the following year.

As we shall see he was a man of many talents and a consummate multi-tasker who could surmount numerous seemingly unrelated issues with ease but those of being a hard-nosed political wheeler-dealer were both alien and indeed probably distasteful to him. Rugby Union in the 1970s and early 1980s was belatedly going through a period of profound change and many of those changes were deeply resented by the current mandarins of the game at Twickenham, Cardiff, Edinburgh and Dublin.

During that period, rugby in Britain had finally allowed the emergence of club knock-out cups but had yet to embrace a system of leagues and the 'elephant in the room' was as always sitting there brooding in the background. This was of course the deeply ingrained paranoia about the imagined horrors of professionalism.

Kendall-Carpenter had grown up, played, taught and administered the game in the strictly amateur 1940s to 1970s environment and had always espoused the sport as being a strictly unpaid one. He firmly believed that a man who had enjoyed playing the game was in some ways honour-bound to give back to the sport and should never accept financial reward for doing so. However, he was far too intelligent a man to simply follow the prevailing wisdom in an unquestioning manner.

As a player he had been many years ahead of his time in thinking deeply about the game and its tactics, formations and skills in an era when even top players frequently just pulled on their kit and boots and went out and did what came more or less naturally to them through accumulated experience. The best players were certainly fitter, faster and had more natural ball skills than inferior ones but still often played the game 'off the cuff' without ever giving much thought to tactics or indeed any concept of individual or group coaching.

In this book I will try to recount his rise from frankly very unpromising beginnings to rugby eminence – the word 'star' hardly applied in that environment – and from there to a leading role in education as the headmaster of no fewer than three well-known schools. At the same time, he had become a prominent member of the Rugby Football Union, initially as the schools' representative before being elected president in 1980 and to then ultimately find himself as the catalyst for the birth of that Webb Ellis Trophy and rugby at last taking to the world stage.

It is now nearly eighty years since his rugby odyssey began and over sixty-five since he stopped playing, so naturally, most of those who played with and against him have since passed away. However, I have had invaluable support from several members of his family, people who were his pupils or staff members at his various schools and a few friends and colleagues who knew him well. I extend my warm gratitude to each and every one of them.

These include his sons Nick and Tim Kendall-Carpenter, who have provided me with a host of scrapbooks, photographs, etc. for which I am particularly indebted, together with John's twin daughters Diana and Elspeth and youngest son Giles. I would also like to thank the following: Jules Boardman, James Bradnock, David Firminger, Mick Hanna, Jill Hooper, Peter Hyatt, John's sister-in-law Philippa Kendall-Carpenter, the late Air Marshal 'Larry' Lamb, Rod Lyon, Peter Michell, Nigel Melville, Lucy Nash, the late Graham Nicholas, Graham Paul, Alan Rogers, Sue Rutherford, Lindsey Simmonds, Geoff Vingoe, Jackie Waters, Phil Westren, the late Alvin Williams, Paul Williamson and Dudley Wood.

I would also like to express my warm appreciation to Sir Bill Beaumont, the chairman of World Rugby, for kindly contributing the foreword to this book.

Finally, I would like to thank my wife, Miquette, and daughter-in-law Kath for their diligent checking and proofreading. This book could never have seen the light of day without them.

1

Early Days

John MacGregor Kendall Kendall-Carpenter CBE. That long name certainly sounds impressive and quite possibly conjures up an image of an aristocratic, wealthy, landowning scion of the establishment born with a silver spoon in his mouth.

This was very far from the truth. When John was born in 1925 the family name was plain 'Carpenter' and even when he began to play rugby he was still regularly referred to as this in the programmes and match reports of the time. According to his eldest son, Tim, there was some understanding reached within the family with regard to including a grandmother's Kendall surname into the now familiar double-barrelled surname. This was only formally adopted by deed poll in 1941.

The second name of MacGregor was a nod to a supposed family line of descent dating back to the Scottish outlaw and folk hero Rob Roy, but throughout his life, John would always regard himself as a proud Cornishman. In point of fact, he first saw the light of day in South Wales where his father was stationed with Trinity House, a service which has provided the country with its lighthouses and lightships dating back to 1514. John's entire connection with Cornwall can be directly attributed to the fact that his father was posted to Penzance where he was to serve on a Light Vessel named the *Stella*.

When you have a name like Claude Eric Kendall-Carpenter you are almost bound to attract nicknames and so his father was generally known in the service as 'Tim', although he also answered to 'Pip', 'Sinbad' and even 'Wee Mac'.

'Tim' was originally from Croydon, had attended Whitgift School and was an extraordinary man in his own right who joined Trinity House as a fifteen-year-old way back in 1906 and remained with them for no fewer than fifty-six years before finally retiring in 1962. His own seagoing career included action in both World Wars. His ship was shelled and he was wounded by fire from a German cruiser named the *Emden* in the First – followed by getting injured again in riots in Ceylon. When recalled home he was sent to northern Russia just prior to the Bolshevik revolution and then, as his convoy returned, was on one of only two ships among a convoy of eight which escaped being sunk by U-boats. If that wasn't enough, he was involved in the fighting at Zeebrugge where he was again wounded and as a result suffered with his right arm for the rest of his life.

A posting to South Wales between the wars was a bit more peaceful and he settled down with his wife Cissie, who bore him three children. Her family tree boasted some notable members including a General as well as a few who were 'something in the city' – as the money men of the Empire were then often referred to. Their eldest child was Frances – generally known as 'Bunty' – followed by John, who came into the world only a few hundred yards from Cardiff Arms Park on 25 September 1925, and finally a younger brother whom they named David. Due to his place of birth, he could, of course, have played for Wales and it was said that when he first came to rugby prominence at Oxford two Welsh selectors turned up at Iffley Road to watch him play. However, they left somewhat unimpressed only to learn afterwards that they had spent their entire afternoon watching the wrong man.

In fact, as that second Christian name MacGregor implies, there was also more than a smattering of Scottish blood in his veins, so he might also arguably have qualified to play for Scotland under today's tortuous qualification rules.

John was still quite small when his father took that posting to Cornwall, where they rented a house in Penzance not far from the railway station. He was not a strong boy but was clearly highly intelligent and it is believed that Cissie taught him at home for much of his early years. She obviously did so very well as he was accepted into Penzance County School when still only eight – some two years early. Had he arrived at the County School a decade or so later he would have automatically been introduced to rugby, but in those days the school only played cricket and soccer – reputedly because the headmaster had broken his nose playing rugby in his youth and considered it all much too rough. Having said that, one other thing counted seriously against young John: he was very, very small.

Once at the County School, he showed an early talent for history – later to be the subject of his Oxford degree – and his school report referred to the fact that he 'learns poetry excellently', which perhaps explains his prodigious memory. He was also in demand for acting on the stage. Not only that but also his high-pitched voice and young cherubic face saw him repeatedly being given the female parts to play. In December 1936, just as the King was renouncing his throne for Mr Wallis Simpson, John was managing to get a lot of laughs from the audience as Cora Golightly in the school's version of *The Midship Maid* and got a very favourable review in the local newspaper *The Cornishman*.

Cissie was, in her own way, almost as adventurous as her husband and when the children were old enough, she used to take them on long cycling holidays around Cornwall and Devon staying in youth hostels. There was much less traffic around in the 1930s and whereas Bunty and John would cycle along by themselves, little David was perched on a carrier behind her.

It was at around this time that John was given his very first rugby ball. One of his father's old Trinity House comrades from South Wales by the name of Jack Evans was also posted to Cornwall as the local Stores Officer. Jack had once played on the wing for Swansea and clearly felt that his friend's son should be 'brought up right' and so gave the young lad the ball to throw around and catch not knowing quite how prophetic his gift would one day be.

Penzance was a quiet, respectable town of just under 20,000 people with an enviable climate but was of course a long way from anywhere else, and the locals saw themselves very much as 'Cornish' rather than English. However, the Carpenters had their sights set a lot wider than just west Cornwall and tried to get John accepted with a scholarship into Christ's Hospital, the famous Blue Coat school near Horsham in Sussex. Sadly, he just missed out, but had he been successful, his rugby career may again have got off the ground several years earlier.

After a couple of years at the County School, John gained a £30 per annum scholarship which helped the family to pay for him to board at Truro School. This was – and indeed still is – a successful independent school in Cornwall's only city. He arrived there for the summer term of 1939, just before the start of the Second World War. Rugby now was one of the sports on offer but, still being very small for his age, this was never likely to be his forte. He was certainly a very long way away from the 6-foot 2-inch and nearly 15-stone Adonis he was eventually destined to become.

One of John's contemporaries at Truro was the future Hollywood film star Robert Shaw of *Jaws* and *The Sting* fame who was to prove a very useful rugby player. The school has continued to produce people with such diverse careers as Sir Patrick Vallance, who was seen regularly on Downing Street Covid broadcasts and Roger Taylor, the drummer of the rock group Queen. Of more relevance was another contemporary of John's at the school who was the towering future second row forward T. K. Vivian. He later played rugby at a high level and ten years later played alongside John at Camborne against the touring All Blacks.

However, the Truro schoolmate who turned out to become a close lifelong friend was another Penzance boy named Harvey Richards. It was Richards who was destined to play a significant role in getting John's rugby career off the ground immediately after the end of the war.

Several years ago, and already into his nineties, Richards recalled how the young Kendall-Carpenter was still a small, rather baby-faced late developer whose voice refused to break until he was deep into his mid-teens. As a result, he was once again prevailed upon to play the female roles in the various school plays which included not only Shakespeare but also J. B. Priestley's *Laburnum Grove* and *Bees on the Boat Deck*.

It was at Truro that John was finally introduced to rugby for the first time and, whilst he showed plenty of spirit, Richards remembered that his sheer lack of size counted heavily against him. John was not only very bright but also an industrious student and gained his School Certificate in 1941 and the Higher a year later. In 1943 he gained his university Higher School Certificate which enabled him to gain a place at Exeter College in Oxford.

The war was still raging although the tide had at last turned against the Nazis and any immediate threat of invasion had mercifully passed. The Americans had belatedly entered the hostilities when John first arrived at the dreaming spires of

Oxford. He had grown slightly by then but was still physically young for his age. Despite the war, there was a little bit of sport going on and so he tried his luck at rugby but, being so small, even Exeter College's Second XV were not impressed and he found himself guesting for Lincoln College's Extra XV.

However, university life at the close of 1943 was very far from normal. John had already developed an interest in flying and had joined the university's Fleet Air Arm's corps. As a result, he soon decided to leave Oxford to volunteer for King and Country – following his school friend Harvey Richards who had recently joined the Navy – and moreover to train as a pilot in the Fleet Air Arm.

Life was now about to change dramatically and become much more exciting. The young man from Penzance was on his way.

2

The Rugby Player Emerges

By the time John joined the Fleet Air Arm at the beginning of 1944, the Second World War had reached a stage that, whilst Britain was no longer in any immediate danger, neither Germany nor indeed Japan was anywhere close to being finally defeated. The Russians had by then halted the Wehrmacht at Stalingrad and Kursk whilst Rommel had at last been chased out of North Africa. Despite this, Normandy had yet to be invaded and the curse of doodlebugs and V2 rockets still lay in the future.

With the United States now Britain's all-powerful ally and being located far from the reach of the Luftwaffe, the USA and Canada were ideal places to train young potential pilots and so John was to find himself gaining his wings in faraway Indiana.

His wartime flying log, courtesy of the Royal Canadian Air Force, has survived to this day and shows that most of his training took place at the Bunker Hill base in Indiana together with a brief period in Texas. His flying training began on 2 September 1944 and he was only finally signed off on 14 August 1945, just the day before the Japanese finally surrendered. He must have had very mixed feelings about this as he had still not fully completed the programme to qualify as a pilot. His passing out certificate quotes that he was a member of Pilots Course 81 which, due to the end of the war, did not complete its training schedule. The log also scrupulously chronicles the fact that he failed one early segment of the programme on take-off and landing as his assessor, a certain Lieutenant Newburg, had climbed into the wrong aeroplane.

He eventually completed no fewer than 250 flying hours of which nearly 100 he had been able to pilot alone. Overall, he had been a diligent, if occasionally devil-may-care student who reputedly did a loop-the-loop (which was strictly banned) on first being allowed to fly solo. He also took full advantage of the hectic social life, absence of blackouts and rationing, sunshine, physical training and last, but by no means least, the huge beef steaks which were always on offer.

Many years ago there used to be advertisements in magazines and newspapers showing a bodybuilder named Charles Atlas who claimed to be able to turn a 'seven stone weakling' into a muscular Adonis if you would only send him a five shillings postal order, and could thereafter have the pick of all the admiring girls on the beach.

The effect of John's year in America was no less dramatic. Having been a late developer physically, he now made up for lost time with a vengeance. He shot up an amazing 6 inches in height to 6 feet and 2 inches and added nearly 5 stones in weight, coming back home slightly under 15 stone. Furthermore, his previously straight blond hair had turned darker and slightly curly. When he arrived back in the UK even his friends and family had to do a double-take before they recognised him. Perhaps it was not quite so surprising in that his younger brother David was destined to top out at around 6 feet 5, but the sudden transformation was nevertheless remarkable.

The war in Europe was by then over and a new Labour government had assumed power by the time John returned to Britain, where he was posted to Cheshire. Although now virtually qualified as a pilot, he had not been called upon to go into action. By August 1945 two atomic bombs had finally crushed even the most fanatical Japanese resistance and so there was now no need to go out and risk death in the Far East. An adventurous young man and being very much his father's son, John would have had mixed feelings about this. This was especially the case as it denied him the opportunity of fully qualifying as a pilot, experiencing some combat flying after undergoing all that training. It also prevented him from being promoted to an officer rank.

On his immediate return he was sent to a camp in north Wales. In one of his letters to his parents he casually mentions playing a bit of rugby, although it was unlikely to have been anything very taxing. On a much more serious note, whilst there he was to meet a very attractive young 'Wren' called Iris Anson who was also stationed in the area serving as a driver. She had a good surname to be attached to the Navy as among her direct antecedents was the famous Admiral of the Fleet George Anson who had circumnavigated the globe capturing Spanish gold back in the 1740s.

She was the youngest in her family, who hailed from the Bromley area, and according to one of her lifelong friends, Jill Hooper, was an accomplished pianist, good at embroidery but hated her Christian name.

> We all still called her Iris whilst we were at school but, by the time she first met up with her future husband, she was always known by her nickname of Toby.

With the war ending, the by now tall, fit and burly young man soon came back home on leave to Cornwall where things of a rugby nature were just beginning to stir in a major way. His home town of Penzance had fielded a rugby team since Victorian times, although until 1945 they had never achieved anything remarkable. Just a mile away, around the picturesque Mount's Bay, lay the large fishing village of Newlyn which proudly boasted a team of its own. They had always had a close and none too friendly rivalry which sometimes broke out into violent matches and occasional fights between opposing supporters to the extent that local fixtures had been broken off on more than one occasion.

War changed many things and compared to all the unspeakable horrors which had taken place around the world, this petty little local grudge seemed rather superfluous. With this in mind, the committees of the two clubs had negotiated both a truce and then a merger and had leased a piece of land known as the Mennaye Field on the edge of Penzance and facing Newlyn to be their new combined ground. It had no facilities whatsoever and had once been an old rubbish tip which had recently been used as a Home Guard and army parade ground where no less than General Eisenhower had recently reviewed some of his massed ranks of GI's before sending them off to Normandy.

The new club was unsurprisingly christened 'Penzance and Newlyn RFC' but, with a passing nod to Gilbert & Sullivan, was affectionately to be known as the 'Pirates'. They had just begun pre-season training when John came home on leave to make a brief visit back to Truro School and to meet up again with his old friend Harvey Richards. Unlike John, Harvey had enjoyed a very successful schoolboy rugby career and had played a lot more during his own wartime service. Meeting up with his now tall and well-built old school pal, he soon had John joining in with the training.

Harvey was selected at fly-half when the Pirates took the field before a packed audience against Guy's Hospital in the club's inaugural match with John looking on as a keen spectator. The Pirates lost but a week later had their first local Cornish match away at Redruth. Unlike the Newlyn or Penzance teams, the 'Reds' had all but dominated Cornish rugby for decades with occasional challenges from Camborne and Falmouth, and another large crowd flooded into Redruth's Recreation Ground.

The story goes that nearing the kick-off the Pirates were still a man short and that the club's ebullient secretary named Rex Carr spotted the tall serviceman who had been seen at training and pressed him into service in the back row. There was to be no fairy-tale ending. John was later to be hailed as one of the great tacticians of the post-war game but at this point he was big, strong and fit but still extremely raw. The Pirates were put firmly in their place by a decisive 24-0 defeat, but this did nothing to dampen his enthusiasm.

Returning to his station, he was able to play a few games of rugby as he and countless thousands of other servicemen at home and abroad waited impatiently to be de-mobbed to pick up the threads of their lives. When he was finally released in mid-1946, he returned to Penzance and reapplied to go back to Oxford and resume his interrupted studies and perhaps play some good class rugby into the bargain. Whilst he waited, he passed the time working as a farmhand hoeing turnips at one shilling an hour, as a lumberjack, and – no doubt influenced by his father – as a deckhand on the *Sevenstones Lightship* between Land's End and the Scilly Isles.

Now in their second season, the Pirates had introduced a Reserves XV, and after a couple of games with them John came in for his second senior match just before Christmas 1946 against a team of Royal Navy Artificers. This time they were much more successful and John topped off a very promising performance by getting one of the Pirates' five tries. Playing alongside him for the first time was Harvey Richards who, now also de-mobbed, was training in London to begin his own long and successful teaching career.

Along with his hard manual labour John trained diligently. One of his teammates was yet another trainee teacher named Geoff Vingoe. At that time Vingoe was a highly rated sprinter at Loughborough College and probably the fastest man at the Pirates. He recalled numerous sprint sessions with John and was astonished at how the much bigger Kendall-Carpenter could match him stride for stride.

It was not just on the training pitch either. Looking back over seventy years the sprinting winger recalled a match now lost in the mists of time.

> Just around Easter we were playing the Old Blues down on the Mennaye. We were losing and back on the defence when my inside partner Mike Terry – who could be a selfish blighter in possession - threw me a looped pass deep inside our own twenty-five-yard line. I took off with a clear run and sprinted flat out to score a try underneath the posts at the Newlyn end of the ground. As I flopped gratefully – and gasping for air – to the turf to claim the try I glanced up and there was John standing over me and he wasn't even breathing heavily!

That 1946-47 season was a key period in John's rugby education and he was a quick learner. One of his earliest games in that period was against a very strong Devonport Services team. In those immediate post-war years when Britain still maintained a large Army, Navy and Air Force – further boosted by thousands of youngsters doing National Service – teams like Devonport could boast numerous international players in their line-ups. That afternoon John had to mark a big rumbustious forward named Brian Vaughan who was destined to pack down alongside him in the England back row when he made his international debut a couple of years later.

But we are getting ahead of ourselves. Having only got into the side just before Christmas, John, despite a cruelly icy winter, managed no fewer than twenty first team matches and played a leading part in the Pirates' first win over Redruth. Enthusiasm for rugby in the area was enormous, partly because with strict rationing in place, no television and very few motor cars, there were hardly any counter attractions.

John kept in touch with Toby and they went to one another's homes for visits but for the time being marriage was not on the cards. Oxford was calling.

During the long, hot summer of 1947, whilst Denis Compton was racking up centuries before lunch at Lords, John was working away on the lightship, training hard and getting ready to return to full-time study. By this time, he was an automatic choice for the Pirates, who had already assembled an attractive fixture list, particularly during September and Easter time when top teams from London and especially Wales enjoyed touring in Cornwall. Before leaving for Oxford, he had already measured his skills against Swansea, Aberavon, Cross Keys and Newbridge and had never yet been found wanting.

All this time he was still generally known in rugby circles as plain John Carpenter and his friends all referred to him as 'Carps' or – if you wanted to be really Cornish about it – 'Boy Jan'. With his blue eyes, slightly tousled brown hair and strong, ultra-fit body Carps was naturally popular, not least with the local young ladies. With peace now fully restored, the armed forces de-mobbed and – despite chronic shortages of just about everything – this was to be a brief, carefree and somewhat idyllic time to be alive.

During those few precious weeks before John resumed university, Penzance had some very important visitors when the Australian Wallabies made it their seaside base before commencing their five-month UK tour with a match against a combined Devon and Cornwall team at Camborne. This match came much too soon for John to have been considered but the visit gave rise to one particular lark in which he would in all probability have played some minor part.

Wallabies captain Bill McLean led a team which included one man of clearly Cornish descent called Tonkin and also a big swarthy prop-cum-lock called Nick Shehadie who nearly forty years later was destined to play a major role with John in establishing the inaugural World Cup. McLean wanted a tame wallaby as a mascot and one was duly provided by Bristol Zoo on the strict understanding it was well fed, watered and closely supervised at all times. Needless to say, one fine evening it escaped and was soon being pursued all over the town by fat policemen, shrieking schoolchildren, dear old ladies and even the fire brigade through houses, gardens, car parks and side streets, before finally being rounded up.

In the meantime, John's rapid progress was not lost on the Cornwall selectors. County rugby in Cornwall was something of a nationalistic obsession and thousands would brave all weathers to cheer on their black- and gold-clad heroes. They also had some powerful talent at their disposal. Dr Keith Scott from Redruth, Devonport's Bill Moore, Penryn's Vic Roberts and big Jim George from Falmouth had all starred for England in that first post-war season. The Rhodesian centre-cum-winger Bob Kennedy, studying at Camborne's acclaimed School of Mines, was soon destined to be capped alongside John as well.

Just after John had re-registered back at Exeter College in Oxford, he was called back to Cornwall to make his County debut against Gloucestershire at Falmouth. John was brought in to replace the unavailable giant that was his old Truro School contemporary T. K. Vivian at what used to be called 'lock forward' but is now generally known as 'Number Eight' with the term 'locks' now referring to those giraffe-like characters packing down in the second row. This of course is the role with which he was to find universal fame but in fact John played at some point in every forward position on the field apart from hooker. His opposing 'Number 8' that afternoon was the highly experienced Bristol stalwart Doug Pratten. John performed creditably enough but Vivian was recalled for the next match against Somerset at Wellington, a small market town between Taunton and Exeter which would later feature hugely in John's future life.

But by then Oxford had taken over his life and it was there that matters really began to develop fast.

3

A Cornishman at Oxford

Exeter College lies in the centre of Oxford close to the world-famous Bodleian Library and owes its name to its founder, the then Bishop of Exeter, when inaugurated back in 1314. The link with Exeter continued as it has also proved something of a magnet for young men from the West Country, and when John returned there in the early autumn of 1947 the entire university was something of a melting pot. Unlike his Cornish predecessor A. L. Rowse, he entered a city which for once had its long history of radical politics mirrored at Westminster where another old Oxford graduate, Clement Attlee, presided over the country's first truly socialist government.

It was in many ways an exciting time to be there. The omnipresent rationing was if anything worse than it had even been during the war itself but the newly found peace still felt wonderful and young people could look forward to a future with seemingly endless possibilities. The intake was a mixture of young school leavers and a large group of older men who had been through the war and now had some serious catching up to do. Some like John had served loyally but had not actually been required to put their lives on the line in combat. Many others came back nursing private nightmares, often with the physical as well as mental scars from being pitched into battle or rotting in enforced idleness in squalid prison camps.

One of these was a fellow Cornishman from Penzance named John Laity who had suffered serious burns in action whilst serving in the Royal Navy. He and John shared a house while they were both at Oxford and he remained one of John's closest friends for the rest of his life.

Exeter College has produced some interesting alumni over the years ranging from J. R. R. Tolkien to Dominic Cummings and in John's era this was no exception. At this early stage, John was still a rather happy-go-lucky young man who was always short of money, loved a party, had an eye for the girls and an enviable capacity for multiple pints of beer. However, just as his body had grown up fast in America, his personality and general outlook would very soon become much more serious.

Whilst at Exeter College John was to rub shoulders with the future world record-miler Roger Bannister with whom he sometimes trained. Drinking large quantities of beer was another happy distraction and it is said that on one occasion he actually broke a record recently held by a young Welshman named Richard Jenkins – as he was then still known – in a boozy Oxford 'sconce', this one apparently involving something like 5 pints of beer going down in one massive gulp. Jenkins of course was soon to become the Hollywood star named Richard Burton. The young aspiring Welsh actor (who was a decent wing forward in his own right) had recently been up at the university on a short non-degree course and had already acquired a reputation for hell-raising when given half a chance.

Young ladies were of course housed in their own colleges and romances had to be undertaken with a fair amount of subterfuge which included clambering through windows left open in the dead of night, scrambling over walls or using secret passages. John was caught red-handed clambering back in on one occasion in broad daylight, which not only got him into some mild trouble but also which – worse still – resulted in a well-known but supposedly secret route becoming permanently blocked off.

John was studying History, which involved much reading and of course an endless stream of essays. His tutor was a gentleman called Greg Barr who happened to also be a stalwart of the Oxford University Rugby Club. As rugby began to take an increasing hold and the demands of training and a cheery social life became ever greater, it would all need a careful balancing act. At least in Barr he would have had a sympathetic ear if an essay had been handed in a bit late.

One of the abiding skills which John soon developed was the ability to multi-task. This became a talent which was to stand him in good stead right up to the end of his life when he had to somehow combine running a large independent school whilst jetting all over the globe setting up a World Cup.

University rugby was at its zenith during the middle part of the twentieth century and Oxford could not only claim the cream of the young boys leaving the various public schools but could also attract plenty of slightly older men like John who had been forced to put both their academic and sporting lives on hold during the hostilities. Furthermore, there was a steady stream of Rhodes Scholars from what was still regarded as the Empire bringing their outstanding rugby and cricketing skills to the university in a steady flow.

As he found his feet back at Exeter College, John found that his money was tight and on a couple of occasions he had to appeal to his parents to send him a postal order for some desperately needed funds. Food was severely rationed and often barely edible but there was plenty of beer and lively company, and inter-college rugby was now far more competitive than it had been in his brief sojourn during the war.

John did not get his 'Blue' in his first full year at university but he did manage to make it into the Greyhounds – Oxford's second string XV – and this brought him into contact with one or two serious forwards. Unusually for the time, they were prepared to give the game and its tactics some serious analytical thought.

One was a tall, rangy and highly intelligent lock from Wavell Wakefield's old *alma mater* Sedbergh named Peter Kininmonth. He was himself destined to play for – and indeed captain – Scotland and also to have a conspicuously successful tour with the British Lions in 1950 in the very slot in the team that John would have loved to have been able to accept. The other was one of those celebrated Rhodes Scholars from Australia called Basil 'Jika' Travers.

Travers was a big, hugely powerful bear of a man who was a full six years older than John. He was already married and moreover had fought the Japanese in New Guinea where he had risen to become a Brigade Major and had already been awarded an OBE for his exploits. Just to cap it all off he was also a first-class cricketer who had taken a couple of wickets off the 1946 Indian tourists when they came to play against Oxford. If you wanted a heroic role model he was your man.

Travers had already played several times for England and was the Oxford skipper in 1947-48 when he led them (without John) against his own countrymen touring as those Wallabies that John had witnessed just a few weeks before down at Camborne. He thought deeply about the game and authored a book on rugby strategy called *Let's Talk Rugger* in 1950 loaded with so many diagrams and arrows as to make it virtually unreadable. For all that, quite a lot of people must have taken it to heart as it was re-issued two years later as *How to Play Rugger*. His tenth chapter entitled 'Forwards in Defence' laid out in detail the art of corner-flagging which was soon to become the hallmark of John's playing fame. Indeed, it set the tone of back-row play for the next couple of decades until changes in the Laws relating to where backs could stand in relation to set pieces led to the 'drift' and 'blitz' tactics of modern defensive play.

This tactic did not lack for critics, many of whom felt that all forwards should be concentrating upon winning the ball in the first place rather than racing away to counteract an opposing move which often might never actually happen. Highly successful back-row men have always courted controversy from the days of Dave Gallaher and his original 1905 All Blacks right up to the modern era of TV commentators becoming apoplectic at the sight of Richie McCaw seemingly getting away with murder on the 'wrong' side of breakdowns. John was soon to attract his fair share of critics as well as admirers as his skills developed.

He had an early taste of playing for the full university side when he made a scoring debut against the Old Merchant Taylors. However, Travers had a few more experienced men to call upon than John but saw him as having a lot of exciting potential. Accordingly, John played mainly for the Greyhounds who boasted a good fixture list in their own right and by the end of the season he had been with them on short tours to Lancashire, South Wales and France and had gained much valuable experience along the way.

Travers certainly made a deep impression upon John. He would run around a practice session armed with a whistle which he would blow and everyone had to stand still wherever they were. He would then castigate some poor unfortunate for being 4 yards out of position. He would also occasionally take a few moments out during a match to stop and think carefully about how the game might be turned around by some subtle change of tactics or perhaps by switching a couple of players around.

Be that is it may, a fertile brain such as John's lapped all this up. After another short Greyhounds tour to Italy, he embarked upon a major long-distance trip for a combined 'Oxbridge' visit to Argentina. As one of the few who had yet to win his 'Blue', John was perforce one of the lesser-known players able to make the long voyage to Buenos Aires and then spend a month playing a total of nine matches finishing with two fixtures against Argentina itself. The tourists recorded a 100 per cent win record and remarkably only conceded eight points in total.

The tourists took a manager with them named Charles Hopwood who was also a Barbarians committee man. The party included neither coach nor medical support but intriguingly their own referee who was a gentleman named Austin Matthews who was destined to officiate in no fewer than seven of the matches. There was a fair sprinkling of both current and near-future international players in the party which was captained by the Scottish lock-cum-prop G. A. 'Gullie' Wilson who had already been elected to lead Oxford University during the forthcoming season.

One of Gullie's decisions was soon to play a very significant part in John's forthcoming rise to being capped for England. The party included not only Peter Kininmonth but also the South African Rhodes Scholar brothers Clive and Tony van Ryneveld and a brilliant young Cambridge full-back who was actually born and bred in Argentina named Barry Holmes. The following season Holmes starred for both Cambridge and England, only to return home to Argentina at the end of the season where he was to die tragically at the age of only twenty-one.

Apart from one easy up country match in Rosario, all the matches took place at the rather old-fashioned wooden stadium Gimnasia y Esgrima in the Plata region of the capital Buenos Aires. These of course included both matches against the Argentinian national team. John did well in his first couple of games and was selected for both 'Internationals', marking his debut with the Oxbridge team's first try. He was selected as a flanker, a position he was later to occupy for both Cornwall and Penzance-Newlyn but curiously never for England.

In many ways the trip had quite a relaxed atmosphere and the Kendall-Carpenter family recount two slightly far-fetched stories relating to his visit there when the young man went somewhat 'off piste' in a way that could certainly never happen today. The first was that John's mother had some relatives who were members of the Plymouth Brethren and had gone out to live in Argentina. Not being required to play for a few days, John accordingly went off to try to meet up with his uncle Charlie who had emigrated out there as a missionary many years before. Having done so he then, according to legend, returned to the party wearing a gaucho hat, poncho and riding a very bad-tempered mule.

The second story sounds equally intriguing. This was 1948 and the high point of the dictatorship of General Juan Peron. His extremely brutal form of national socialism made him a natural ally for the likes of Franco in Spain and he gave shelter to a whole rag-bag of ex-Nazis on the run from the Allies. His glamorous radio star wife was of course the world-famous Evita who was introduced to the touring players. Allegedly she took rather a shine to the handsome young

Cornishman and invited him for a ride in her private plane. John was aware enough to realise that getting tangled up with the wife of a fascist dictator with a dubious reputation for torturing and shooting people was probably not a good career move and politely declined!

The tour only ended on 5 September and so by the time the team had landed back in England, it was time for the new season to begin.

4

The Big Breakthrough

For most students the second year of a three-year degree is the most fondly remembered. Friendships, often to last a lifetime, have already been forged, all the best local watering holes have by then become cosily familiar and that looming day of reckoning when Final exams have to be faced is still a comforting distance over the horizon.

It is also a time when non-academic pursuits, be they political, romantic, musical, religious or sporting, can be given free rein. John had come back from Argentina with his rugby reputation greatly enhanced and although he had still to earn his 'Blue' in the annual date at Twickenham with Cambridge, surely it was now merely a matter of time.

As we have seen, Gullie Wilson had already been elected as the Oxford captain before leading the combined Oxbridge team to Argentina. The role of captain carried vastly more power and responsibility than in today's environment of specialist coaches, medical staff, conditioners, video analysts and dieticians. Essentially, he was in charge of everything other than the fixture list which would have already been decided a couple of years in advance. He picked the team, planned and led the training, decided the tactics and motivated his players. A 'secretary' was also elected from among the senior players who could provide logistical support, but all ultimately fell upon the captain.

Gullie had seen enough on the summer tour to be certain to want John somewhere in his pack but the question remained as to where best to play him. John was big, strong, deceptively fast, could leap like a salmon in a lineout and, apart from his tours to Italy and South America, was by then a county player with Cornwall. Gullie already had three fine back row men in Kininmonth, Gill and Tony van Ryneveld plus Nelies Vintcent – a tall South African lineout specialist – to accompany him in the second row but found himself very low on available props. Could this versatile Cornishman do a job for him?

The role of a prop forward in the late 1940s was very different from that expected today. They were usually short, squat and extremely strong. The ball had to come into a scrum more or less straight and a skilful hooker could dominate possession for his team given the large number of scrums awarded for the frequent handling errors committed by exclusively amateur players. He could only achieve this if he was flanked by two virtually immovable objects with broad shoulders that he could swing upon. Such was the lot of the typical post-war prop. Generally, they were not expected to do a lot of running with the ball, pulling off flying tackles or scoring tries. This was seen as the sole prerogative of the 'glamour boys' in the threequarters or perhaps those speedy chaps in the back row.

These prop forwards were not only extremely tough but also there were dozens of tricks of the trade which had to be learned – often the hard way – before anyone could be considered to be anything like the genuine article. Unlike today, the Varsity match was then considered the next best thing to playing for England or Scotland and the competition in the set pieces out on the pitch would be unrelenting. Could this athletic young man make such a major transition in just a few short weeks?

Gullie pulled in a couple of tough, well-known experienced club props to test him out on the training field but one match convinced not only Wilson but also John himself that the answer was a resounding 'yes'. It came on a cold autumn Tuesday afternoon at Oxford's Iffley Road when Cardiff came up to play.

In 1948 Cardiff could, with considerable justification, claim to be not only the best club team in the British Isles but also arguably in the entire world. They had a dazzling group of star backs comprising of Bleddyn Williams, Dr Jack Matthews, Frank Trott, Les Williams and Billy Cleaver. In front of them they boasted a fearsome pack which included Wales prop Cliff Davies, hooker Maldwyn James, lock hard man Bill Tamplin and wily back row men in Les Manfield and Gwyn Evans. If all this wasn't enough, they were led by the great scrum-half Haydn Tanner who, although by then soon to retire, was generally recognised as the best Wales had ever produced – at least until a certain Gareth Edwards came along twenty years later.

The crowd was treated to a rare old battle which surprisingly finished as a 0-0 draw. Such a scoreline tends to indicate a pretty boring afternoon but this time it couldn't have been more different as Trott and Cleaver probed the corners and Oxford's flying centre Lewis Cannell was hauled down by Bleddyn Williams only inches from the line. The forward battle was a revelation and, according to *Daily Express* rugby journalist Pat Marshall, Oxford actually won the scrum battle.

> Cardiff couldn't beat Oxford in the set scrum. Oxford won the set scrums 19-10, nor could they match them in the lineouts where Nieles Vintcent, Gullie Wilson and John Carpenter were superb.

Another rugby scribe of that time was Laurie Pignon of the *Daily Sketch* who went one step further to forecast,

> Vintcent and Carpenter are not only certain to get their Blues but after yesterday's match - watched by an England selector - they should receive invitations to the first England Trial.

In fact, that first Trial took place before the Varsity match and therefore no university players were included as they were saving themselves for the big day, which finally dawned on Tuesday 7 December. By then John – still generally referred to as 'J. K. Carpenter' rather than the double-barrelled version – had undergone another thorough examination of his propping credentials when the university just went down to a star-studded Major Stanley's XV which included a large contingent of English, Irish and indeed French international players.

The big day duly arrived and some 45,000 expectant fans filed through the Twickenham turnstiles, and they were treated to a thrilling match. With a heavier pack and prompted by the South African fly-half Murray Hofmeyr (who was later to represent England as a full-back), Oxford controlled the first half and changed ends with an 11-0 lead. Cambridge came back strongly in the second half and the Dark Blues had to mount a sustained period of desperate defence to finally run out winners by 14 points to 8.

After some suitably raucous celebrations, the team then crossed over to France and gave Stade Francais a sound beating in Paris by 28-3 during which John claimed one of the tries.

Now things were beginning to move very fast. As Laurie Pignon had prophesised, the England selectors had by then taken a good look at John as a possible for the future. They were also very much on the look-out for some new props. The hard-nosed old Coventry prop Harry Walker was a tough, durable character (he lived on to reach the ripe old age of one hundred) but was of the old school and had been playing senior rugby since before the war.

The previous season his final England propping partner had been a burly Gloucestershire loose-head called Tom Price from Cheltenham. Others who had been tried alongside Walker had included Bedford's Geoff Kelly and George Gibbs of Bristol, and the selectors had even turned to Sale's hooker Eric Evans as a makeshift prop against Australia. His particular glory days alongside John were yet to come.

As luck would have it, the second trial featuring the 'Probables' versus the 'Possibles' was to take place the following weekend and furthermore, it would be back down in Cornwall at Camborne. John was joined in the 'Possibles' pack by fellow Cornishmen Vic Roberts and Jim George, both of whom had by then already played for England. It was one of those typical misty December afternoons in Cornwall and it was a somewhat scrappy affair although that Argentinian-born full-back Barry Holmes managed to look like a true star in the making.

John did well enough to warrant a second chance and New Year's Day 1949 saw him back at Twickenham representing 'The Rest' against what the selectors considered to be their putative England XV. Once again, the weather was vile; the wind howled and the rain lashed down. Then suddenly it miraculously stopped and the sun shone briefly but benevolently on the thirty extremely muddy rugby players.

The Rest pack had been doing well playing into the elements and were winning the majority of the scrums, which always bodes well for front row men. During that ten-minute spell of sunshine, the underdogs then suddenly struck and scored two unanswered tries to throw all the selectors' plans up in the air.

One was credited to the Harlequin flanker Ted Horsfall and the other was to be snapped up by John. Props back then were viewed as mere beasts of burden and weren't really expected to score tries, and furthermore an England XV was not supposed to be turned over by 'The Rest'. It was all getting very interesting.

Over the weekend the selectors finally made their choices for the forthcoming match against Wales a fortnight later in Cardiff. The Rest front row of Mike Berridge, Peter Henderson and John had done the business at the Trial and two of them were to be included in the England team.

The unlucky one was John.

5

Your Country Needs You

In mid-January England took the field in Cardiff with no fewer than nine players becoming capped for the very first time. The selectors had originally plumped for recalling Jika Travers who had been one of the few who had stood out in the Twickenham washout, but he had then been forced to withdraw with an injury.

England held on at 3-3 until half-time but were then undone by the sparkling skills of Glyn Davies who had appeared for Cambridge in the Varsity match six weeks earlier and had inspired the Light Blues' brave comeback in the second half. Plied with pinpoint passes by the astute Haydn Tanner, he twice sent the flying Les Williams scorching over for two superb tries. Indeed, it was an afternoon for speedy wingers as, in addition to Williams, both Ken Jones for Wales and Jack Gregory for England were Olympic-class sprinters in athletics. Furthermore, the Welsh front row established a clear ascendency in the set scrums, so the England selectors had some more head scratching to do.

When the next team to face the Irish in Dublin was announced no fewer than six changes were made and one of them was the omission of Mike Berridge for John, who was now named in the front row and finally credited with his full name of J. MacG. K. Kendall-Carpenter. He was to be joined by three more men from Cornwall in Vic Roberts of Penryn, lock Jim George from Falmouth and that Rhodesian mining student named Bob Kennedy on the wing.

Intriguingly the selectors somehow couldn't make their minds up about the back row, naming Vic Roberts and Brian Vaughan but then announcing that shadowy figure who often appeared in programmes of the day – 'A. N. Other' – obviously hoping that Travers would be declared fit in time. As the trip to Ireland drew near, he was clearly still not going to make it. In the event Berridge was given a second chance and John was moved to make his debut back in his already favourite position in the middle of the back row.

The Republic of Ireland in the years after the Second World War was very different from that which it has become in recent years. The divide between north and south was if anything even more acute. It is a remarkable testimony to the spirit and ethos of rugby that two doctors of different Christian faiths in skipper Karl Mullen from the south and the little genius fly-half Jack Kyle from Belfast could play happily together in a completely united Irish XV and indeed later tour for many months as soulmates with the British Lions.

The Republic of Ireland had stayed out of the war and many English and indeed Scots and Welshmen were not very happy with the stance they had taken. Certainly, they had avoided all the bombing and food rationing, but life in the Republic was still hard, wages were desperately low and a combination of President Eamon De Valera and the ultra-conservative Roman Catholic archbishops ruled the country with something of an iron fist.

Irish rugby tended to be a reflection of its society. The sport itself ran a poor third if not fourth behind Gaelic football and hurling with soccer also having a significant following, especially in Dublin itself. Irish forwards were typically rumbustious – occasionally a bit wild – but often lacked organisation and physical fitness when asked to perform at the very top level. A very different approach from that of John.

For all of that the Irish were going to be a real handful. Not for nothing were they the reigning Five Nations champions having just claimed the Grand Slam for the very first time following an epic win against Wales in Belfast the previous March. No fewer than seven of that Grand Slam pack had been selected again and thus they clearly knew how to win. There was also an uncomfortable memory for the English in that, on their previous trip to Lansdowne Road a mere two years earlier, they had been thrashed by five tries to nil as the Irish celebrated a crushing 22-0 win.

Once again England were beaten fair and square by 14 points to 5 with Jack Kyle proving to be the star of the show. As for John's debut performance, it could be said that, although he had been forced to change from being a prop where all his recent rugby had been played, he had adapted exceptionally well.

Writing in the *Daily Telegraph*, the cricket/rugby journalist E. W. Swanton commented,

> Carpenter though unpractised as a backrow forward, did some useful salvage. He prevented one try by his speed in getting back to fall on the ball.

A fortnight later the French came to Twickenham and few gave England much of a chance of beating them. Since the Wallabies had won comprehensively at Twickenham some fourteen months earlier, England's recent record was dismal – played seven: drawn one: lost six.

France could call on some exciting players, not least their 'glamour boy' winger Michel Pomathios, a highly talented full-back in Alvarez and two outstanding back row men in Jean Prat and their skipper Guy Basquet. They also boasted a couple of huge, rock-hard lumps in the second row named Soro and Moga. Even their surnames seemed to conjure up the crack of doom!

As for England, Jika Travers was now fit to play and John reverted to his front row place where he was selected alongside a new hooker. This was a medical student named John Steeds whose England career was notable in that he was the first man ever to have been capped from the Saracens. They were then just a relatively modest club tucked away in the suburbs of North London.

England made an explosive start. Steeds heeled from the first scrum for fly-half Ivor Preece to skip away drawing the French defenders before sending a perfect pass to his centre Lew Cannell who sliced through to score by the posts. The stunned crowd rubbed their eyes in disbelief. There was one man sprinting alongside the flying centre ready for the pass that was never needed. It was a prop forward who had shot out of the scrum; it was of course John.

At a subsequent lineout Travers sought out Moga, the big French enforcer, and whacked him. The big Frenchman went down, was too stunned to retaliate and the psychological force was now clearly with England's pack. As the game progressed, they became ever more dominant as John and his fellow prop Tom Price came out well on top of their opposite numbers.

Suddenly all doors seemed to be bursting open as the following week John received his first invitation to play for the Barbarians at Bedford in the annual match celebrating the memory of First World War hero Edgar Mobbs. He had alongside him both Tom Price and hooker Peter Henderson in a powerful team led by Haydn Tanner.

The Barbarians have been a national rugby institution for almost as long as the game has been played. An invitation to play for them has, until very recently, been considered one of the highest accolades in the sport. Founded back in 1890, it had a remarkable record of longevity among its committee and indeed the president at the time of John's debut was an elderly gentleman by the name of Emile de Lissa who had been an active member of the club since the time of the Boer War. He had never been much of a rugby player himself but most of the other committee members had played at a significant level generally dating back to around the time of the First World War.

They had no home ground and their fixtures followed a repeating pattern of six matches a season starting with a Boxing Day game against Leicester, that East Midlands match in early March and ending with an Easter tour of four games in South Wales. They were always based at a Victorian hotel in the seaside town of Penarth known as the 'Esplanade' from where they faced the local club every Good Friday. It was a cheery, supportive gathering with a clear emphasis being placed upon flowing, attractive rugby rather than on the actual match result.

They also had a well-worn mantra that 'The Barbarians are for good sportsmen of every class but not for a bad sportsman of any class.' As a result, there were quite a few miners and farmers who fitted in perfectly happily with the public school and Varsity types but, in the still class-ridden England of the time, an Oxford man like John would have found it a particularly congenial environment.

Suffice to say the Barbarians won that initial Mobbs Memorial match comfortably enough, scoring six tries in the process, and John was embarking upon an extended and very happy association with them.

England's final challenge was the Calcutta Cup match against Scotland back at Twickenham. For once the selectors picked an unchanged team and John took his place again against a Scottish pack which included his Oxford teammates

Kininmonth and Gullie Wilson. At long last the England team were able to cut loose in the second half to cruise to a five tries to none victory.

It had hardly been a vintage season having lost both their away games before their two Twickenham victories. On the other hand, English supporters had particularly enjoyed the form of the talented Oxford centres Van Ryneveld and Cannell plus the outstanding talent of the ill-fated Barry Holmes. For his part John was seen as remarkable for the extraordinary all-round ability he had shown over and above the basic scrummaging duties of a top-level prop.

Going home to Penzance for the Easter holidays he returned to the back row for a couple of matches with the Pirates which included a game against Cardiff. This took place in front of a large crowd of local supporters who were taking great pride in their own 'Boy Jan' becoming the town's first England player since way back before the First World War.

By coincidence his next match took place over the actual Easter weekend and found him pitted for a third time against Cardiff. This time it was in front of a throng of over 40,000 fans, once again in the famous black and white shirt of the Barbarians. He also had a third match for them in a 6-3 win at Rodney Parade against Newport. It was a typically enjoyable Barbarian Easter trip with plenty of fun and games, Sunday golf and the chance to meet up in a totally relaxed manner with men who had been trying to knock the living daylights out of one another in an international match only a few weeks earlier. What wasn't quite so typical was that the 'Baa-Baas' somehow managed to win all four of their matches.

Just to round off his holiday he was back in Wales yet again, this time with the Pirates playing at Cross Keys before returning to Cornwall, stopping off on the way for a match against Bath. He would have had no idea that this was the club which was destined to play a major role in his career within just a few years.

As he went back to Oxford for the summer term, he could reflect upon a period of not more than six months during which he had catapulted from relative obscurity to becoming a major 'name' on the British rugby scene. Journalists had by then largely stopped referring to him merely as 'Carpenter' and had now begun to give him his full name.

A summer free from rugby was both an opportunity to catch up with his history studies and also to spend a bit more time with the young lady in his life, Toby. With John being based at either Oxford or Penzance and she living in East Sussex, this was obviously not as easy as either of them would have liked but they somehow kept close until they finally married once he had obtained a settled job and a regular salary teaching at Clifton.

All this however was still a little way into the future.

6

Player and Leader

It is now well over half a century since John Kendall-Carpenter was playing the game and the sport has changed significantly since that time. This is particularly true with regard to those performing at the elite level. The most obvious aspects of this came with the advent of professionalism but this did not occur in any formal sense until five years after his premature death in 1990.

John repeatedly spoke out against what he perceived as the dangers of paying men to play rugby and in fact even argued against rugby being played on Sundays, something that has been going on regularly in England since just after he gave up playing. It must be stressed that he was a highly educated man with a mind which could accommodate a wide variety of views and ideas. He thought deeply about the game and how it could not only be played tactically but also was perfectly capable of seeing merit in several aspects of Rugby League. This was at a time when such a stance was viewed as almost heretical in the more closed minds of virtually everyone involved in the Union game.

He was a big enough man to be able to cut through much of the hypocrisy and snobbery and see the sport in its essentials of running, handling, tackling and physical confrontation that both codes embodied and could envisage numerous ways in which his own Union code could be improved. Obsessed with kicking, scrum-halves repeatedly worked their way up and down touchlines leading to endless, often chaotic lineouts. At a set piece both sets of backs were allowed to encroach almost right up to one another, thus neutralising most of the space required to move the ball. These were just two aspects of the game which frequently spoiled matches – if not for the players themselves they certainly did so for spectators. Many subsequent developments of the Laws – although certainly not all – can be argued to have greatly improved the game both as a spectacle and indeed for players' enjoyment.

Rugby League had long since dispensed with the lineout entirely dating back to its infancy. Union had retained them and it was an aspect of the game at which John excelled. During the past twenty-five years lineouts have been much better controlled with the lifting of jumpers not only allowed but also actively encouraged. This has resulted in a much better structured game than one where players had to constantly contend with all the pushing, shoving and brawling that seemed to happen every time the ball was thrown in, which was the case when John was playing.

Throughout his long playing and administrative career John never harboured any resentment towards those who openly went over to play League as a profession. However, he always had a deeply held sense of honesty and thus found some of the shenanigans involving certain Union players receiving what was euphemistically called 'boot money' deeply offensive. It wasn't the amounts involved – which were usually quite small – but that it was all just so 'grubby'.

Graham Paul was a talented young fly-half from Penzance who was just setting out on his career with the Pirates as John's playing days were drawing to a close and who then went on to play for Cornwall for a couple of years. When still quite young he decided to join Hull Kingston Rovers in the Rugby League who converted him into a winger. From here he scored boatloads of tries and actually represented Great Britain.

Many years later, long after they had both ceased playing, they found themselves together acting as judges at a local Penzance school sports day. Graham recalled a fascinating couple of hours sitting in the sunshine where they discussed all the relative merits of both codes and that he was amazed at how John seemed to understand immediately many of the finer tactical aspects of Rugby League. This was at a time when John had by then become a committee member of the all-powerful Rugby Union and Graham was still being barred from entering the Pirates club on the basis that he had once committed the apparently heinous crime of providing for his family.

When it came down to tactics in his own Union game, John soon acquired a reputation for being something of a guru of his time. Newspaper columnists were soon repeatedly referring to him as 'the most knowledgeable man in the game'. Whether this was justified or not is immaterial; the fact was he had both an instinctive and a theoretical 'feel' for what worked on the field and what did not.

A man with a fertile rugby brain appears to have an inbuilt radar system which allows him to arrive at the right place at precisely the right moment. Even when he had just started playing seriously, and indeed before he had started back at Oxford, he seemed to have the gift of strolling into a space and being in precisely the right position as the play came back to him as if miraculously drawn by a magnet. His old Pirates captain Bill Monckton once apparently referred to this gift as 'educated idleness' which seemed to sum it up nicely. As one looks at the old grainy newspaper photos of the time it is uncanny how often two or three players are engaged in a tackle and there, just a few feet away in the background, John can be seen ready to pounce and intervene.

His physical abilities of course were needed to get him to wherever that rugby brain was telling him to go, as instanced by that try-saving swoop in his first England match in Dublin or appearing alongside Lew Cannell as he swept in for his early try against France. The term 'backing up' was widely used at the time and referred to being in the right place to support the ball carrier so that he could pass or offload the ball as he was about to be tackled. This skill needed both the mental capacity to anticipate precisely where to run as well as the pace and stamina to actually get there.

Those physical abilities were in themselves extraordinary, particularly given his late development as a teenager. There was of course no question of any coaching when he first arrived to play for England but the players were allowed a single stiff runout on the day before an international match. This generally involved a few lineout drills, the backs practising some running and passing and perhaps the centres would try out a scissors move or two. At the end of this, all fifteen players lined up on the practice pitch goal line in their rugby kit and boots and sprinted to the far posts. One of the wingers was Bristol's Jack Gregory who the previous summer had been a member of Great Britain's 4 x 100 yards relay team at the London Olympics, and he predictably came in first. However just a yard behind him in second place was the new boy Kendall-Carpenter who had been originally picked as a prop.

Another art in which he excelled was jumping high to take the ball in those rough-and-tumble lineouts which, as mentioned, could not be assisted - at least within the current Laws – by anyone lifting him. John stood at 6 feet 2 inches, which of course would be considered a back row midget today, but he was blessed with both a remarkable spring and the shoulder strength to withstand plenty of buffeting whilst in the air.

Another Pirates player of the same vintage as Graham Paul was a tough and athletic second row forward called Alvin Williams who was the same height as John, a St Luke's College PE student and nearly ten years younger. He recalled a training session at the Pirates not long before John's eventual retirement which ended with players pairing off to do a few exercises together. Alvin was challenged by John to leap in the air and clap his hands above the crossbar. Try as he might, Alvin could only just touch the bar and was rather put out when the older man could perform the crossbar hand-clap with comparative ease. Of course, modern lock forwards can do this very easily but then most of them are 6 feet 7 or taller and have spent countless hours in a gym doing leg presses and jumping with weights.

The tactic for which he is best known is what was popularly known at the time as 'corner flagging'. While this had been espoused by Jika Travers and had already been widely adopted by back row men since before the war, it was John who turned it into something of a science. As with any defensive tactic, it had its outspoken critics and detractors but nobody could gainsay its effectiveness.

Under the Laws of the time backs were allowed to line up at set pieces far closer than today and a top-class centre such as Bleddyn Williams of Wales or Jeff Butterfield of England became stars as they possessed the God-given ability to sidestep through and could then feed the fast men outside them. They would then go flat-out along the touchline to either crash over by the corner flag or, if possible, run round to dot the ball down by the posts to enable an easy conversion.

The role of the fly-half was either to straighten up the line and pass, kick for touch, nudge through a short 'grubber' kick into the space behind the opposing back line or – most thrilling of all – to cut inside his opposite number when he could then sprint away from defenders and leave an open field for those outside him. In John's era men like Ireland's Jack Kyle, Glyn Davies and Cliff Morgan of Wales and England's Martin Regan were the past masters of this. Of a slightly more recent vintage Barry John, Phil Bennett and currently Marcus Smith at the Harlequins also come to mind.

His main enemy was the opposing wing forward who would come flying off the side of a scrum or the back of a lineout and hopefully either smash the fly-half into the turf or – if that was not possible – to force him outwards, thus cluttering up the midfield and crowding his centres who then would have to either stop or even backpedal in order to maintain contact. In this way they became easier prey for their opposing centres flying up to tackle them.

However, if the line was indeed breached or the ball was grubber-kicked through there was only a full-back and hopefully a covering winger to provide any meaningful defence. Furthermore, the defending forwards had to disengage themselves from the scrum, ruck or brawling lineout and thus could offer very little defensive support for those vital few seconds until they had struggled back.

A 'corner flagger' if he was fast enough and a sufficiently accurate tackler could offer a different solution. Essentially, he would fly off the back of the set piece but, instead of chasing the opposing fly-half whom he would leave to the tender mercy of an aggressive flanker, he would sprint across the field behind his own threequarters and hopefully be there to crash any potential try-scorer to the ground or into touch. That was the theory anyway and if you had the pace and anticipation with which John was blessed it could be extremely effective. This was to be amply demonstrated to the wider rugby public in the next forthcoming Varsity match.

As your thinking man's rugby player, John was soon to be called upon to captain the various teams he played for. In due course he was to not only lead England for a spell, but also Oxford, Cornwall, the Barbarians, Bath and the combined Oxbridge team which toured South Africa when he was probably at the very peak of his powers.

As with everything in rugby, he gave the role of the captain some considerable thought. In a 1963 interview in *Rugby World*, several years after he had ceased playing, he expounded his ideas about captaincy in the days long before a coach would predetermine most of what was expected out on the pitch.

Asked about handling difficult personalities in a team his response showed a surprisingly light touch.

> I know you come across some awkward characters. Ballerinas I call them but you have to get them on your side. Talk to them, make them think that what comes out of your mouth is their decision. Handle them like pieces of Dresden China.
>
> One of the most arduous tasks facing a skipper is of course the need to preserve a fighting spirit - even after setbacks – during the heat of battle.

Asked about how he tackled this aspect he stated,

> By positive, but infrequent intervention. There is the type of skipper who clenches his fist and shouts about having 'more blood on our boots' but

this tends to insult their intelligence and usually peters out after about ten minutes.

As to off-the-field communication his thoughts were,

> Before the game and on the field, I was the boss but after the final whistle I mucked in as much as possible and got to know my men. However, be careful as an unconsidered comment of yours in a pub may go around very fast and assume such proportions that a lot of damage is done. If you are not ready to say something profound or important, then say something trivial or futile.

As for the two best captains he felt he had played under, he considered them to be Gullie Wilson back at Oxford and Sale's Eric Evans who had a way of knowing quickly what made each of his men tick. Then, just a few minutes before a match kicked off, Evans would bring out a carefully measured bit of the old 'God, King Harry and St George' stuff to wind them all up enough to then go out ready to die for the red rose on their England shirts.

By the time John returned to Oxford in October 1949 much of this was already crystallising in his mind and his future looked particularly bright.

7

The Flying Prop

As the new season came around John was facing up to two major challenges. Firstly, to pass his final exams so that he could, at long last, claim his degree some seven years after he had first arrived at Oxford as a young teenager halfway through the war. He, like hundreds – if not thousands – of other young undergraduates had served loyally in the armed forces but now had to make up for lost time and get on with their chosen careers, get married, start families and finally become part of the real world.

Secondly, having tasted international rugby, he certainly wanted to experience a lot more of it and gaining a second 'Blue' was not only the best route to doing so but also was a very important ambition in itself. On form this was something he was virtually certain to achieve but he would have to continue to devote many hours away from his studies and of course stay away from injury. In later life he was to describe university rugby as perhaps the zenith of his career, even eclipsing his exploits with the Barbarians and England. This would seem odd to modern rugby followers but at that time no other rugby match anywhere compared in terms of targeted preparation, practice and the demand for peak physical fitness.

He began the season with half a dozen matches in the back row for the Pirates which included a notable victory over Blackheath. He also featured in a couple of games for Cornwall against the British Police and Gloucestershire. The game with Gloucestershire was a hard-fought draw at Redruth with John packing down in the back row with his England colleague Vic Roberts and the blond St Ives flanker Tony Bone. This particular third row of the scrum was generally considered to be Cornwall's best and, whenever they were all available, they represented Cornwall together throughout the early 1950s.

At Redruth they had all but carried Cornwall to a memorable win when, in the very last moments of the match, Cornwall were penalised whereupon Gloucestershire's full-back Bill Hook drop-kicked a massive 55-yard goal to equalise and in so doing bring himself to the close attention of England selectors.

John knew he had to study extremely hard for his exams, which for some reason resulted in him briefly losing nearly 2 stone in weight. This presented something of a crisis as it was unclear whether he had simply been overworking for a vital forthcoming exam and not eating enough or whether he was carrying some mysterious virus. Either way he had to pull out of the Oxford team for several matches.

Then by a happy turn of fate, and perhaps because Oxford rarely had any examinations in the autumn, that worrying exam was delayed. John relaxed and, as if by magic, most of the weight and strength piled back on again. If he was due to prop a scrum in a Varsity match, he would have been hard put to have done so down at around 13 stone, even at that time when top-level props were generally at least 20 per cent lighter than they are today

If there were any doubts about his strength and fitness these were answered completely by mid-November when he excelled in helping the university to a close victory over another powerful Major Stanley's XV during which he was able to more than hold his own against his propping England colleague Tom Price. Just before half-time any of those lingering concerns were instantly dispelled when, as the *Daily Telegraph* reported,

From a kick-off Carpenter followed up fast and led a grand rush which ended with Curtis touching down.

and again, in the *Daily Express,*

John Carpenter was the inspiration of the Oxford forwards. The tall tousle-headed Cornwall and England front row man covered the ground so quickly that he was as good as any wing-forward on the field.

By now he had come to the Varsity match and the single incident which was to propel him headlong into national rugby fame and how, even seventy years later, old-timers and rugby historians still refer to the incident.

These matches were always desperately hard-fought encounters and the 60,000 spectators had endured a rather scrappy match. The only score had been a slightly fortuitous try by the Oxford lock G. N. Gent who was able to drop on a ball which had squirmed over the try line following a mistake among the Cambridge backs.

The two sets of forwards had enjoyed a tremendous battle with John – once again appearing as a prop – having been much to the fore. As the final whistle approached, the two packs had seemingly fought themselves to a virtual standstill. The pale winter light was fading fast when Oxford full-back Murray Hofmeyr for once missed touch with a towering kick into the sky, whereupon it was pocketed by Cambridge's Glyn Davies who sent his centre John V. Smith off on a searing break up the middle. He swept past his opposing England international centres, Boobbyer and Cannell, then performed a sweeping sidestep past the despairing Hofmeyr to finally shoot away upon a lung-bursting flat-out sprint for the corner.

The thousands of Cambridge supporters in the crowd suddenly leaped to their feet and roared him on as exhausted Oxford defenders raced back across the field in a desperate but futile attempt to cut him off. Just as Smith was preparing to dive over in the corner to either draw the match – or even win it – a dark blue shirt hurled itself at him and smashed him over the touchline just inches from the corner flag.

This time the Oxford supporters and true rugby fans throughout the old stadium screamed with excitement and cheered themselves hoarse at the sheer drama of it all. As the two men staggered to their feet it was clear that the man who had made that incredible tackle after nearly eighty gruelling minutes of toil was none other than a prop – John.

It was said that the then Prime Minister, Clement Attlee, a devoted Oxford man who had studied Law at University College some forty years before, was in the crowd and in his excitement hurled his homburg hat high into the air in sheer delight and it was never seen again! One of John's future colleagues at the Pirates was a young curly-headed scrum-half named Peter Michell who had been taken along with some of his school teammates by his headmaster at Wycliffe College to see the match as a special treat. He recalled,

> Being from Penzance and having seen him play several times at the Pirates I already knew a fair bit about him but for all that we could hardly believe our eyes.

In his *Daily Express* report the following day their sports reporter, Jim Swanton, described it well.

> This was a grand effort by Smith and a scarcely less one by a front-row forward in the 79th minute of the hardest of games. Also, as some remembered it was an indirect triumph for B. H. Travers, that insatiable theorist, who these last few years never ceased to drum into Oxford forwards the vital importance of corner-flagging.

The champagne and beer flowed that night as the partying began in earnest but there was an amusing sideline to the celebrations. Despite continued food rationing Nelies Vintcent, Oxford's tall South African skipper, had decided that in the interests of team bonding, there should be a gargantuan feast just a couple of days before the big match.

Fortified by lots of extra goodies sent in by loving families from overseas, the lads all tucked in with a will, no doubt accompanied by a great deal to drink. Come the day, notwithstanding John's epic last-ditch tackle, several of the pack were deemed to have struggled.

John vowed there and then that would not happen again next year if he had anything to do with it.

8

England Expects while the Lions Hope

The Dark Blues celebrated their last-gasp victory and then embarked upon a short pre-Christmas tour to the south of France, opening with a narrow defeat in front of 15,000 spectators at Toulon but following up with victories over Grenoble and Lyon.

For John the combined pressures of cramming for his Finals and maintaining his England place were only just beginning. Just to add to the conundrum, the British Lions were due to tour New Zealand and Australia that summer having not done so for twenty years. Although it was still early days, the Home Nations selection panel would already have had a 'long list' of potential tourists and the name of 'Kendall-Carpenter' would undoubtedly have been somewhere on it.

The first hurdle was an England Trial at Gloucester for which John was selected in the front row for the 'Probables' team alongside future England leader Eric Evans and Wally Holmes from the Nuneaton club. There was always a degree of controversy whenever Trials teams were announced and this time it tended to centre around the selection of no fewer than four South Africans – all of whom were studying at Oxford.

Looking back, it is interesting to reflect on the policy of selection at the time. A very large contingent invariably came from the armed forces, the teaching hospitals and the two leading universities. However, via the still-vibrant County Championship, there were still opportunities for men from some of the lesser-known clubs such as the Nuneaton-based Wally Holmes and the tall second row Todd from Penrith RFC up in Cumbria. The Trial went off satisfactorily enough and John retained his place in the prospective 'England XV' to take on the 'The Rest' a week into the New Year.

Before that there was another welcome invitation from the Barbarians to play in their annual Boxing Day encounter at Leicester. He had the by now familiar company of Price and Ginger Steeds in the front row and his lofty South African Oxford colleague Nelies Vintcent pushing behind him from the second row. Those matches were often tightly fought affairs with Leicester frequently winning in front of 20,000-plus supporters at Welford Road. This time the

Barbarians won quite easily by a 29-0 scoreline but one would imagine that with the Internationals only three weeks away, avoiding injury would also have been high on players' minds.

With the Final Trial successfully overcome, John was duly named in the England team to face Wales at Twickenham. Although lacking the injured Bleddyn Williams, it was still a very talented Welsh team which had been assembled. It would duly go forward to win the Grand Slam (although it had yet to be referred to by that term for a few more years) and to provide at least half of the entire Lions party the following summer.

A record crowd of over 75,000 squeezed into Twickenham and witnessed an early try for John Smith making his debut and having clearly got over any sense of disappointment following John's last-dich tackle a few weeks before. However, prompted and inspired by the young prodigy Lewis Jones at full-back, the Welsh slowly took a vice-like grip on the match and, as the second half progressed, the hordes of visiting Welshmen began to engulf the rather rickety old stadium in song. John battled away up front, won some useful lineout ball but it was just not going to be England's day.

Three weeks later the Irish came to Twickenham. Selectors almost invariably wielded the axe after any sort of defeat and Evans, Rimmer, Vaughan, Hofmeyr, the pack leader Hosking and the Waterloo flanker John Cain were all given the chop. John would have been pleased to see his fellow Cornishman Vic Roberts back as the open side wing forward and Steeds was restored as hooker at the expense of Eric Evans. It was Roberts who claimed the only score of yet another close match when he picked up a loose ball about 25 yards out to fling himself over the line despite a crashing tackle from an Irish winger.

Once again John had done well in the lineouts and had held his own in the scrums against a broth of a boy from Young Munster called Tom Clifford. Then, as now, they bred them tough down in Munster and the story goes that after John's debut the previous winter Tom had regaled the 'innocent' young student John about how he was lucky to have been moved to the back row. Had he remained at prop, Tom would have stuck his thumb in one of his eyes when the ball came in.

This time they indeed came face to face and it is said that at the very first scrum John jabbed his thumb hard into one of Tom's eyes and enquired 'Is this what you meant?'. True or apocryphal, this illustrates that, whilst he might have been a Varsity man with high values of sportsmanship, he was not about to be bullied or intimidated by anybody.

Now came a point when an important decision had to be taken. As mentioned, exams would have to come first and the Lions were due to leave for New Zealand before Easter with their first fixture set for 10 May and, moreover, they were going to travel by sea. In a perfect world, being able to follow up university Finals with a Lions tour could make sense and those exams generally took place in early May. In more recent years and with the easy availability of jet travel a man in John's position could have sat his exams and then flown out to join the party just a week or so into the tour. This has since been the case with several exam takers selected for a trip to New Zealand which include Mike Gibson and Gerald Davies. Even with air travel in those old propellor-driven planes, the journey could have been achieved in about three to four days, as replacement Lewis Jones was very soon to prove.

Rugby authorities were notoriously inflexible at the best of times and, having decided that the party would all travel together by sea, they were not going to make any exceptions. To be fair, air travel in the decade after the war was still considered rather dangerous and it was also felt that the time spent at sea would enable the players to bond with one another. So, unless they were to call for a replacement among the forwards, playing for the Lions was going to be the one major rugby honour to elude John.

He was not alone as the non-flying embargo ruled out both Lewis Cannell and Brian Boobbyer plus the Welsh captain John Gwilliam and Scotland's outstanding loose forward Doug Elliot as well. The big Scottish farmer was so keen to be included that he had actually offered to pay his own air fares only to be rebuffed by the 'powers that be'.

Another longer-term issue had needed to be resolved and that was what was he going to do as a career once he had graduated. If he was going to marry Toby and provide properly for her, how was he going to earn his living? As a young Oxford graduate who had served during the war and now a rugby player of some renown, he could undoubtedly have picked up a not-too-demanding job in those days of full employment. He might well have joined one of the big organisations like ICI or Shell (which employed Eric Evans) as a management trainee without much difficulty and any number of companies would have loved to have him in their sales force – but what did he actually *want* to do?

His mother had a number of family connections in the Stock Exchange but somehow the prospect of a bowler hat with rolled umbrella and catching the 8.05 each morning from Reigate or somewhere similar held very little appeal. Furthermore, he was still only twenty-five and could potentially look forward to another five or six years of top-level rugby. This would rule out any potential overseas commercial postings which were still the norm for young men on the lower rungs of a career ladder in the large British companies. The more he thought about it the warmer he felt towards the idea of the teaching profession.

There was one other potential benefit and that was that he could take another year at Oxford gaining his postgraduate teaching qualification. By the time the 1950 Five Nations competition had begun he had accepted the onerous role of captaining his university during the following season. This would fit in nicely with studying back at Oxford during the autumn and then going out to a school doing teaching practice during the latter part of the academic year.

In actual fact he was very soon lined up with a job for when he had finally qualified, which was as a junior master at Clifton College near Bristol. In his pocket he had a letter from its headmaster as early as April 1950 formally offering him the position which he could take up as of September 1951. This was nearly eighteen months into the future and was obviously based upon the assumption that he would successfully obtain his Diploma of Education.

Clifton's headmaster Desmond Lee was an eminent academic in Classical Philosophy but was clearly anxious to recruit a young sportsman of John's standing. Despite the fact that teaching included Saturday mornings, his offer letter made it quite clear that his new recruit could disappear to play rugby more or less as and when required.

The next England fixture involved the attractions of a visit to Paris. Despite beating the Irish there was some further tinkering by the selectors as they restored Hofmeyr as full-back at the expense of Waterloo's Bob Uren who had himself just been brought back after two years in the wilderness – only to then be promptly dropped once again. The main headlines however were reserved for the sensational inclusion of Wellingborough schoolboy Johnny Hyde who had recently been tearing up the wing for Northampton. Still happily alive at the time of writing, he was only destined to be capped twice over a three-week period and hence his international career was at an end when still a few months short of his twentieth birthday, thus surely making him one of the youngest 'has-beens' in rugby history.

England's pack was left unchanged and this match marked the last occasion John would be required to play for his country as a prop. His direct opponent was the equally versatile Rene Bienes from Cognac who, like John, would play much of his distinguished career for France in the back row. Heavy rain had left the pitch at Stade Colombes very wet and greasy and the spectacle suffered as a result.

In his book on England rugby, author John Griffiths comments that, 'Hofmeyr was reliable and he received valuable support from Small and Kendall-Carpenter.' Despite their efforts, the French probably deserved to secure a narrow victory by two unconverted tries to one.

Given that he was already destined to lead Oxford for the following season and as events were to unfold England as well, John got an early taste of captaincy when the Barbarians invited him to skipper their team in his second Mobbs match back at its usual venue at Northampton. Tellingly, he was also picked to play back in his favourite position in the back row alongside his Oxford and England teammate Harry Small and another Oxford man, Philip Moore. Moore was destined to earn his solitary England cap ten months later on a day when John had to pull out of an England team for the one and only time in his life.

The final match of the season was the annual Calcutta Cup, this time in front of 70,000 enthralled Scotsmen at Murrayfield. For this match Coventry's lofty Stan Adkins was moved up into the second row, thus allowing John to occupy the Number 8 position – although in those days it was often given shirt Number 14 when teams usually lined up with the Number 1 being given to the full-back. This berth in the middle of the back row was now to be his for the next four years.

Again, the weather was wet and blustery but the referee, Captain Dowling of Ireland, allowed the players to express themselves and as a result the large crowd could enjoy not only a rare Scottish victory but also a much more exciting game of five tries with the result in doubt right up to the final whistle.

Very soon the British Lions, which eventually included a mere three Englishmen, were to embark upon their long voyage to New Zealand leaving John behind to face those all-important Final examinations. He was successful and obtained his degree although he later confessed to a little bit of good fortune in a key History paper. He was cramming up to the very last minute and was still doing so on the bus going to the exam itself. The thing he was reading happened to be about the repeal of the Corn Laws and – lo and behold – it came up and he was thus able to declaim on all the arguments of Cobden and Bright with commendable authority.

We all need a bit of luck occasionally and a little Cornish piskey can come in very useful sometimes.

9

Captain of Oxford

Having successfully completed his exams (gaining a good Second Class Honours in History), John was able to relax a little, spend more time with Toby and enjoy the sunshine and beaches back in Cornwall. His parents were still based happily in Penzance but moved house several times before finally settling in one near to the station. Meanwhile his father was still working hard for Trinity House and continued to do so for another decade.

Reports on the Lions trickled back from New Zealand and John no doubt secretly envied Lewis Jones. The young Welsh national serviceman stationed at Devonport received an urgent cable inviting him to cross the world in a succession of aircraft to join the Lions where he was an immediate sensational success.

Cornwall in the decade after the war still had precious little in the way of entertainment to offer young people who nearly all had jobs and at last a little pocket money to spend. In the summer you could go mackerel fishing or brave the infuriating tar which sullied all the beaches but, after dark, opportunities were very limited. Cornwall as yet still had no television, only the wealthy and farmers had cars and , unlike today, there wasn't a restaurant worthy of the name for miles around. Crowds often numbering in the thousands would regularly flock to watch the Pirates where he would be a star attraction on the rare occasions he was at home from Oxford to play for them.

Apart from that, Penzance had its pubs of course, three cinemas and a dance hall on the promenade known as the Winter Gardens. John was at that time still a bachelor, he was by then undoubtedly famous and a 6-foot 2-inch, blue-eyed hunk as well, and so in that insular environment he was probably the nearest thing to a rock star you were ever likely to meet. Not surprisingly the local lasses would be drawn towards him like moths around a light bulb. What – if anything – he did about it shall remain in that rusty old rugby filing cabinet clearly marked 'What goes on tour...'

In fact, by the time a man reaches the age of twenty-five his character has become largely formed for the rest of his life. His daughter Elspeth kindly managed to dig out a copy of the university magazine *Isis* from that autumn in

1950 written as he prepared the team for his third and final Varsity match. The author – who clearly knew him quite well – attempted to sum up John's now developed personality in a few paragraphs:

> There is no doubt that he has grown out of his boisterousness and that he is more mature than most of his Oxford contemporaries. It is a solid maturity which includes a life outside his rugger and University activities – not the apparent preoccupation with the cares and problems of the political world which so often passes for maturity in Oxford.
>
> He is at once a restrained and forceful personality, eager and calm. John is a fit leader, one that does not dally over non-essentials, whose only fad is his deliberate shunning of fads. He is efficient in business and alert at committee meetings. And on these qualities, he has been elected president of his Junior Common Room.
>
> It is unfair to analyse John too thoroughly. The essential unity of the man defies it. Accept him as you find him and let him grow on you. He will keep his distance according to his will - not yours. He will always find himself in a position to deal a powerful slating even to his fellow rugby stars, if he considers it necessary; and not even the enormous knowledge of the game which the other Internationals in the team possess will shake the strength of his decisions. His self-confidence is justified.
>
> To all but a few, John is somewhat uncommunicative and only a handful know him well.

To all this we can add his already extraordinary ability to undertake in twenty-four hours what most people would need an entire week to do, a strong sympathy for the underdog and being a man who did not suffer fools gladly. Indeed, in later life he was able to largely ignore any criticism from people whom he did not admire or empathise with which could sometimes convey a certain remoteness to those who did not really get to know him. To those who did so he was invariably a true and steadfast friend.

Despite all the Cornish summer attractions and with an eye firmly fixed on his forthcoming captaincy duties at Oxford, he made certain that his fitness levels were as high – if not higher – than they had ever been. The arrival of September saw him embark upon a tumultuous merry-go-round of matches which included four for the Pirates and several 'Invitation XV' matches which were very popular with rugby followers at that time before the League system was brought in and swept them all away.

At the risk of repetition, the role of a university captain in those days before the advent of coaches was an extremely onerous one and again bears no relation to captaincy in the modern era. As already mentioned, he would have been expected to decide upon tactics, select the team, tell unhappy players that they were being dropped, supervise all the training, arrange various social events and talk to the press. All of this came on top of maintaining his own form and fitness in order to lead by example. He knew exactly what he was letting himself in for having seen at close hand Travers, Wilson and Vintcent all performing the role in their own individual ways.

Given Oxford's penchant for recruiting highly talented 'colonials' on scholarships he was destined to be the first Englishman to lead the university since before the war. He also had good reason to be confident in the knowledge that he had a good number of experienced men to call upon, many of whom were already international players in their own right.

This was particularly true in the backs where he could select men of the calibre of Cannell, Hofmeyr, Boobbyer and the Kiwi wing Ian Botting of England, Laurie Gloag of Scotland and the young cricketer Chris Winn who would also soon be playing on the wing for England. Having determined that he would now be playing all his rugby in the back row, he could again call upon Harry Small and the soon to be capped Chris Rittson-Thomas to join him. Furthermore, two of his front row colleagues from the previous year – Emms and Hefer – were also available once more.

For all that he did not have an easy ride up to the Varsity match itself. For a start Murray Hofmeyr, who had been elected Oxford's cricket captain for the 1951 summer, had decided he should stop rugby for the time being and concentrate on actually doing some work. It took all John's persuasive skills to get him to change his mind but the gifted South African did not appear until the Stanley's match deep into November and only a few short weeks before the Twickenham match itself.

By this time John's fame had spread far and wide although the modern 'celeb' culture was still decades into the future. The largely West Country students at Exeter College and those from the predominantly Welsh backgrounds at Jesus had developed a long-standing rivalry which occasionally resulted in them playing rather childish tricks on each other. John had popped into Jesus College to meet a friend and soon found himself surrounded by noisy students who promptly took him hostage. Word quickly got out and a contingent from Exeter set out to rescue him and soon a mini-riot took place.

One of the leaders of the kidnapping party was a young American Rhodes scholar by the name of Stansfield Turner. A quarter of a century later Turner was appointed Director of the CIA by President Jimmy Carter having previously headed up NATO in Europe. When the burly John had refused to come quietly, Turner merely remarked drily 'Next time we take a hostage we will have to choose someone a bit smaller.'

Back on the training pitch, John was struggling to find suitable men for certain key positions and in all no fewer than twenty-six players were tried. He even had to play again as a prop in an encouraging 11-6 win over a powerful Cardiff team which was just seeing the emergence of a youthful Cliff Morgan as its exciting prospect at fly-half. As to his leadership the correspondent for *'The Times'* remarked that,

> Kendall-Carpenter kept his men well together during the crises in the second half when Tamplin and his men were threatening to break loose.

Repeated reference has already been made to John's remarkable ability to multi-task and this was amply illustrated on that particular afternoon. The Cardiff fixture took place on the very same day that John was finally to receive his MA degree from the Dean of Exeter College at the historic Sheldonian. He somehow managed to receive his degree with appropriate decorum, rip off his academic cap and gown and leap into a waiting taxi to speed him off to Iffley Road just in the nick of time for the kick-off. History doesn't relate whether he was wearing his jockstrap and rugby shorts under all that academic regalia but it would be no great surprise if he had.

Whilst early term results were encouraging, a spate of injuries disrupted matters and disappointing defeats were suffered at the hands of Blackheath and also Richmond, whom Cambridge had defeated on the previous weekend. Fortunately, Hofmeyr was now persuaded to dig out his rugby boots and the England full-back with the astute rugby brain took over the reins of the key fly-half position which had caused John a succession of major headaches.

Major Stanley's fielded an exceptionally strong team that season with every single one of them being from the British Lions party recently returned from their summer tour. There was a fascinating battle between the two back rows and John received numerous plaudits for how he had led from the front as the Oxford trio rampaged around the park throwing multiple spanners into the works of their celebrated opponents.

Suffice to say that, thanks to the promptings of Hofmeyr and the outstanding dash of Chris Winn, Oxford won a famous victory. The large crowd contained a good contingent of England selectors who could not have failed to see how well John had led from the front when they were mulling over who might be the England captain after Christmas.

This was followed up a few days later by another fine performance to overcome the Harlequins at Twickenham despite now having both Winn and Cannell added to the injury list. John capped another fine performance when he scored a try from using his pace to get up alongside a clean break by his scrum-half and dive over in the corner.

With regard to leadership, the venerable rugby scribe Dai Gent commented that,

> Once again the forwards from the start faced up to this strong Harlequins pack and had the better of the tussle with their captain Kendall-Carpenter keeping them well together and every man going his hardest.

When John led Oxford out onto the Twickenham turf for the Varsity match itself there was little doubt in the minds of most of the pundits that they were the clear favourites to win. The pitch was still firm from overnight frost and covered by a light dusting of December snow. Oxford nearly scored almost from the kick-off but Lew Cannell was forced into touch at the vital moment just before touching down. Hofmeyr kicked a penalty but then suffered a painful groin injury although, with no replacements allowed, he gamely carried on having reverted to his normal position at full-back. This now presented John with a severe captaincy challenge.

Full-back had been one of his most difficult problem positions all through the autumn and he had finally plumped for another young and relatively inexperienced South African called Davies. He had a back line loaded with

England players but somebody had to supply them with sufficient ball for them to do their stuff. So, with a slightly dodgy full-back now having to play out of position in the key fly-half spot and Hofmeyr clearly in considerable pain, the team began to struggle.

Fortunately, his forwards were able to answer John's call to arms and tore into Cambridge. Oxford's hooker Hefer managed to dominate the scrums and the lanky Walker surpassed all expectations in the lineouts. Hofmeyr had been given a painkilling injection in his groin and John tried him briefly again at fly-half, but he was clearly playing in some distress. The tension was lifted when Brian Boobbyer sidestepped his way through the Light Blue's defence to provide prop forward Emms with a try to settle matters. Therefore, John had completed his Oxford career by being the winning captain and with three Varsity wins out of three.

It was nearly time to move on.

10

Being England's Leader

Just before the Varsity match the England selectors had assembled at Otley near Leeds for the first of three Trials. Naturally no university men were included but they had seen fit to include both centre-threequarters from the Pirates in a team they called 'The Whites'. Selectors always seemed to demonstrate a form of tortured logic that ordinary folk found impossible to comprehend. Although they picked one of them, John 'Ginger' Williams, in his proper position, they perversely selected his friend Mike Terry (whose mid-field defence in particular exceeded Ginger's) out on the wing where he had hardly ever played before. Poor Terry never got a usable pass during the entire match and was never given another chance.

A second Trial at Taunton was snowed off but two were subsequently held at Twickenham. John was handed the captaincy of the 'Probables' but it turned into one of those selectorial disasters when the underdogs comprehensively stuffed the presumed senior team by four tries to one. The axe was bound to fall and several good players (including the talented Chris Winn) were tossed aside but fortunately they kept faith with John. A second pointless – in both senses of the word – match also took place at Twickenham and now it was time to come up with the final selection.

At this point it is perhaps worth recalling the environment in which an international skipper was expected to operate. Rugby Union was then, and indeed continued to be, run very much on hierarchical grounds very much like the armed forces. The committee men were very much the 'officers' and their word was invariably the law whilst the players – including the captain – were definitely in the 'other ranks' and when it came to selection, they were invariably treated like cannon fodder.

Most of the players were still of an age where they had either served in the war itself or had at least done, or were about to undertake, a period of National Service. For this reason, and despite five years of post-war socialism which had rejected much of those old master-servant type attitudes, the majority of rugby players continued to accept this state of affairs without undue complaint.

Even the captain only knew if he was selected when a little postcard arrived in his letterbox or if he happened to see it in the stop press column of an evening newspaper. There was no question of any coaching being allowed and of course – unlike cricket – he had no say whatsoever in who might be in the team he was expected to lead. If he managed to hold onto the job for a few seasons like Karl Mullen in Ireland or Guy Basquet in France, he might develop some sort of rapport with his men and have a good idea of their relative capabilities but, with the notable exception of Eric Evans just after John bowed out, this was never allowed to happen with England.

The selection system on this occasion was even more of a farce than usual. The elected chairman was Surgeon-Captain Osborne who had recently managed the Wales-dominated Lions in New Zealand and thus presumably knew a great deal more about all the Welsh players than the English ones. Just to add to the Mad Hatter's Tea Party, he was unable to attend that awful final trial as he was bedridden with flu. The other four selectors had somehow managed to cobble together a provisional team through a succession of phone calls culminating in a proposed fifteen being submitted to Captain Osborne by a letter in the post.

Be that as it may, when they finally announced the team to face Wales, John was duly named as captain in a team which included no fewer than nine men who would be making their debuts. Conversely Wales could boast one of their finest ever teams with the vast majority having toured with the Lions and thus had a degree of confidence and mutual understanding that England's collection of relative greenhorns could never hope to match.

Just to add to the difficulties the match was due to be played at Swansea rather than Cardiff and 50,000 noisy West Walians were not likely to give their white-shirted visitors very much in the way of sympathy.

One of the selected back row men only gained the one cap but went on to achieve much greater things far away from the rugby field and this was John's Barbarians colleague Philip Moore. He had preceded John at Oxford before embarking upon a stellar career in the Civil Service, becoming Private Secretary to the Queen and retiring as Baron Moore of Wolvercote with a grace-and-favour apartment in Hampton Court Palace. In due course John himself would become a CBE and a Bard of Cornwall but even he could never quite match that.

John must have viewed his team's prospects with some foreboding but then he was also struck down with flu and had to withdraw. His career saw him turn out to play with a broken nose, wired-up teeth and myriad other injuries but flu was something which could lay even the strongest athlete flat on his back. The battered England selectors brought in yet another new cap in Chris Rittson-Thomas from John's Oxford team but decided to wait to decide who would lead this somewhat motley crew when they all got aboard the train at Paddington. The obvious choice would have been Coventry's Ivor Preece who had already done the job the previous season and had toured with the Lions. But no, after a lot of head scratching they somewhat perversely then awarded it to John's Cornish compatriot Vic Roberts instead.

The result was entirely predictable and England were heavily defeated although they defended courageously against a very confident Welsh team in which Lewis Jones was able to turn on the style for his army of adoring supporters.

John probably felt a pang of guilt in not being able to lead his men in this thankless task but from a career point of view it was probably a very good game to have missed. Nevertheless, he was back and in charge again for the trip to Dublin where of course he had begun his England career two years earlier. He returned at Number 8 at the expense of Philip Moore and among several changes he was able to welcome his Penzance teammate Ginger Williams.

After the Swansea fiasco things had got rather better organised and the team went over an extra day early and had a decent practice session at College Park. John's old scrapbook also contains a touching good luck telegram from Toby back working at a school at Seaford in Sussex.

John's first game as England's leader was certainly no classic and was lost by the unpromising score of a single penalty goal to nil. By all accounts it was rather more exciting than it sounds with England twice being thwarted by last ditch tackles and the new fly-half Evan Hardy rattling an upright with a drop goal attempt from fully 50 yards. Ginger Williams also distinguished himself with a timely interception of a pass right in front of his own posts when the great Jack Kyle seemed certain to score.

John's personal performance was generally applauded in the press despite the fact that he received a really bad facial injury but played on. Irish forward play at the time could probably be described as 'robust' rather than overly scientific. Unlike the carefully orchestrated 'catch and drive' and rolling maul of the professional era the green-shirted warriors of the day loved nothing better than a wild foot-rush which had all the characteristics of a death-or-glory cavalry charge and they were never too bothered where they placed their feet. It took a brave man to dive on the ball in front of one of those.

At one point, John did precisely that and got a stray boot in the face for his trouble. Of course, he played on whilst spitting blood out of his mouth completely ignoring the fact that two of his front teeth had been smashed off at the roots. The man from the *Daily Telegraph* was clearly impressed.

> The real star of the English pack was Kendall-Carpenter. Never can he have played a better game. He was always ready to break away on his own and the manner in which he repeatedly popped up in defence to save extremely awkward situations was astounding.

It was now the turn of France to come to Twickenham for a match that was to be dominated by Jean Prat who was their star flanker from Lourdes. That little town in the south-west of France is of course world-famous for the shrine of St Bernadette and the thousands of pilgrims who flock there every year in the fervent hope of curing the sick. In the 1950s it also boasted a truly outstanding rugby team.

If the match were to be played in the modern era there is absolutely no chance that John would have been allowed to participate. After the Dublin match it became clear that he had not only said goodbye to a couple of teeth but also his jaw had been broken in two places and had needed to be wired up. Having already missed the match in Swansea there was no way he was going to miss out for a second time for a little thing like a broken jaw.

Nobody in their right mind would decry the present-day system of Head Injury Assessments (HIAs) and enforced layoffs for players who have been knocked out and by today's standards leading out England a mere fortnight after breaking one's jaw would seem foolhardy in the extreme. On the other hand, that generation of men had been through the war and had seen many far worse things and took it all in their stride. Sadly, in an era long before the introduction of replacements during a match, many brave players had done themselves terrible long-term damage by exacerbating injuries through staying out on the pitch when they clearly should never have been allowed to have done so.

The crowd was smaller than usual due to a rail strike and France had never yet won in London, but now they were to do so by two tries, a conversion and a penalty to a single try for England by Boobbyer. Once again injuries played their part with both Rittson-Thomas and full-back Hewitt being off the field for lengthy spells. Given the circumstances, it was understandable that the talented French scrum-half Gerard Dufau enjoyed a particularly productive afternoon and, although England hung on bravely, they were finally killed off by a towering drop goal from Monsieur Prat.

John's face survived the ordeal and on the following Monday morning a telling photograph appeared on the back of *The Times*. It featured a French winger being hauled down about 2 yards from the English line by his opposite number. There, just behind them on the try line itself, was John no more than a few feet away ready to pounce whilst the rest of the England pack can be seen puffing back some 20 yards behind the play. If ever a picture encapsulated John's art of corner-flagging this was surely the one.

Despite the fact that John had done as much as anyone could have ever expected, the brutal point remained that England's results that season under his leadership had been somewhere between dire and bloody awful. Three matches played and three lost – with only the Irish match being even close – hardly smacked of success and England were marooned at the bottom of the Five Nations table.

The final chance to salvage some national pride came with the Scots coming down to Twickenham. Yet again the desperate selectors chopped and changed, recalling Ginger Williams and partnering him in the centre with a man called Alan Towell from Bedford whose only previous cap had been three years earlier when England had been soundly trounced in Paris.

They had wisely decided to bring together fly-half Evan Hardy with his regular Blackheath and Army scrum-half partner Dennis Shuttleworth and restore the Northampton firebrand Don White to join John and Vic Roberts in the back row. White was a larger-than-life character on the rugby scene and had actually made his England debut in the very first peacetime International back in 1947.

This time the changes brought about success and all of the men brought in acquitted themselves extremely well. The fact still remained that the 5-3 victory that was gained was only down to new full-back Bill Hook's conversion of Don White's opportunist try when he jumped upon a heel from the Scotland scrum to sell an outrageous dummy and plough over the line.

Under the headline 'Fiery England Forwards' correspondent Dark Blue was fulsome in his praise for John's performance.

> Kendall-Carpenter, the English captain, is to be congratulated on the way he kept his pack going to the finish. He himself was often a conspicuous figure at the lines-out and his huge left-footed punts often saved awkward situations.

This was all extremely gratifying and possibly bordered upon flattery but for all of that – and despite playing three more seasons of England rugby – he was never asked to lead an England team again.

11

Chasing the Springbok

Before the season drew to a close there was another delightful Barbarians tour of South Wales. Once again, John appeared against both Cardiff and Newport but, unlike his previous visit, both matches were lost. By this time he had become something of a Barbarian regular having also featured in the Leicester match over the Christmas holiday.

Within a few days he was to pack down for a second time against Cardiff, this time with rather more success. Whenever possible he would get in some club rugby and this naturally involved returning to Cornwall and his beloved Pirates. Each April Cardiff would send a powerful team down to Penzance for what was usually considered to be the glamour match of the season. Not surprisingly their team, with a liberal sprinkling of Welsh international stars, was usually a bit too strong for their ambitious hosts but the previous April the Pirates had surprised everyone – including themselves – by pulling off a shock victory.

As expected, a huge crowd surrounded the touchlines at the club's Mennaye Field which saw John in his usual Number 8 position being faced by the rising Wales star that was Sid Judd. It was a titanic struggle which ended in a breathless 3-3 draw courtesy of a try by centre Mike Terry – the man who had been so misused by the England selectors up at Otley just a few months earlier.

Before the season ended, John played several more matches for the Pirates alongside his old friend from Truro School Harvey Richards, culminating in a brief appearance back at Twickenham where the club had been invited as a guest team in the Middlesex Sevens. It was indeed extremely brief as they were knocked out by St Thomas's Hospital in the very first round!

John could then look forward to a period of four months before he was required to report for duty at Clifton and this was a window of opportunity which could certainly not be wasted. That summer London was due to celebrate the emergence from the war with the Festival of Britain which was a welcome fillip to the country's morale. For John, recalling the success of the combined Oxbridge tour to Argentina three years earlier, another far more ambitious tour was planned – this time to South Africa.

Once again, the party was led by Charles Hopwood with John as the obvious choice as captain. Although they took only twenty-three players, he was able to call upon ten men who had already represented their countries and five of the party had grown up and learned their rugby in South Africa which was clearly going to prove very useful.

Rugby in South Africa was at the time very much an 'all white' affair and New Zealand touring teams had somewhat cravenly seen fit to avoid selecting any players with Māori or Pacific Island heritage whenever they visited. By 1951, the South African Nationalist party had only come into power three years before but had already begun to enshrine their already long-standing strict racial discrimination practices into what was to then become the notorious apartheid laws.

The South African style of rugby was based upon powerful scrummaging and, with a steady stream of immensely strong Boer farmers readily available, they had plenty of the right men to carry it out. Although the Oxbridge team were of course students by definition, they were virtually all fully matured men of whom many had already served in the Armed Forces. Fortunately, all of their ten fixtures were to be against various university combinations rather than those battle-scarred cattle ranchers from the Transvaal.

Having backs available of the pace and quality of Cannell, Boobbyer, Smith and Winn, it was clearly to the Oxbridge team's advantage to generate a fast and open style of play wherever they could and for their backs to lie deeper than usual in order to generate more space for themselves. South African crowds responded enthusiastically, seeing this as a welcome change from the more sterile forward-dominated fare which had been their usual diet.

The first match took place at Durban's Kings Park at the end of July and, despite going down 5-8 to the University of Natal, the tourists made a profoundly favourable impression with local Natal newspaper man Tom Meehan reporting how 'Kendall-Carpenter, the visiting captain and fittest man in their pack showed fine positional play.'

The tour continued across the country playing to gratifyingly large and enthusiastic crowds and featured well-attended matches at all the major Test venues. These included Loftus Versfeld at Pretoria, Ellis Park at Johannesburg, Newlands at Cape Town and of course Stellenbosch University which was the home base of South African rugby's uncrowned king Dr Danie Craven.

Whilst up on the Rand the party made a visit to a gold mine at which they were shown a foot-long ingot of solid gold. Given its weight their guide challenged the tourists with the task that if anyone could pick up the gold bar with just one hand, he could keep it. True to form, John volunteered and – equally true to form – lifted it high into the air in one large mitt. The poor guide nearly fainted on the spot and a couple of security guards seemed to be fingering their revolvers, at which point John handed it back saying 'That was just a joke wasn't it.' The trembling guide looked extremely relieved.

The tour ended with a respectable return of three wins, three losses and four draws from their ten fixtures and had been watched by over 150,000 spectators despite several of the lesser games taking place at relatively small venues. With a small squad John had been required to play in every single match and more than once had to select himself in the front row in order to cover for the inevitable injuries.

As the 2021 Lions found to their cost, the South African press corps, rather like their New Zealand counterparts, can often be accused of being unduly harsh on visiting tourists – especially ones from the UK. However, this time they were spontaneously generous in their assessments and were unstinting in their praise for John's own powers of leadership, physical fitness and in particular his prowess as a lineout jumper. Indeed, the *Transvaal Sunday Times* published an iconic picture of John towering above an opposing second row forward Ernst Dinkelmann – soon to be one of the lineout stars of the Springboks' upcoming tour of Great Britain.

Each year the South African media would honour five outstanding rugby stars of the season and that year they proudly selected the bald flanker Basie Van Wyk, burly prop Chris Koch, lock 'Salty' du Rand and full-back Johnny Buchler. The fifth place might have been expected to go to the blond Hennie Muller, nicknamed the *'windhund'* (greyhound), whose phenomenal pace around the park was to be such a feature when the 'Boks arrived in Britain. But they didn't; they named John Kendall-Carpenter.

With the coming of the autumn, the Springboks were scheduled to undertake a full-length tour to the British Isles and France having not done so for twenty years. They had played very little rugby at a Test level for some considerable time mainly due to the war and were thus something of an unknown quantity. There had been a single visit by New Zealand in 1949 when they had been well beaten to the tune of four tests to none by their South African hosts and since then the All Blacks had defeated the British Lions. If that was going to be any sort of a guide, one would expect them to be well-nigh unbeatable even away from their own home turf.

Despite all his experiences to date, John had yet to play against a major touring team in Britain having not yet broken through to rugby prominence when the last such team – the 1947-8 Wallabies – visited the United Kingdom. The Springboks' ship docked at Tilbury hard on the heels of the returning Oxbridge students and the tour was quickly up and running.

As usual John now had to balance several spinning plates at once as he had just begun his career as a junior master at Clifton. The second match of the Springbok tour in early October was to be against a combined Devon, Cornwall and Dorset-Wilts team at Home Park, the still bomb-scarred football stadium of Plymouth Argyle. As the most recent England captain it would have been fairly natural that he should have been called upon to lead the side but such combined teams were nearly always selected upon political compromises.

With Plymouth being situated just over the river in Devon, it was the practice that the fifteen players would be comprised of seven from Devon and seven from Cornwall plus one lonely soul from Salisbury representing Dorset-Wilts. Furthermore, Devon would be expected to supply the skipper and this honour fell to the weighty Barnstaple lock Bert Jones. To be fair he was a recent England player and a fine hard forward in his own right but it does demonstrate just how banal team selection processes were at the time and indeed continued to be so for another twenty years.

On a happier note, John had his Cornish compatriots Roberts and Bone beside him in the back row and his Pirates colleague Ginger Williams in the centre plus the intriguing prospect of the Woodgate brothers together up front.

Billy and Eddie Woodgate were a pair of identical twin props from the Devon seaside town of Paignton who were not only two very tough hombres but also had a disarming way of confusing referees who might have already warned one or the other for some piece of skulduggery. They would invariably claim after a further offence that 'It wasn't me Sir I think it must have been my brother.' They also looked out for one another so, if ever an opponent had a bit of a contretemps with one twin, he would probably need eyes in the back of his head looking out for the other.

The game itself was very hard fought and was much closer than the 17-8 score in favour of the Boks might suggest with the big difference being the superb goal-kicking of their chunky prop forward Okey Geffin who landed four penalties and a conversion. Although John was not leading the team, he once again dominated the lineouts against the very large Springboks' jumpers Pickard and Dannhauser and employed what at the time was considered an unusual tactic of having flankers Bone and Roberts packing onto the second rather than the third row of the scrum. This had the effect of slowing down the Springbok heel, tying the flying Hennie Muller into the scrums and thus denying the tourists one of their most potent attacking weapons. This is a clear example of how John's tactical approach to a game of rugby was beginning to pay huge dividends and to earn him that flattering title as 'the most knowledgeable man in the game'.

His second meeting with the Boks came at the beginning of January when England faced them at Twickenham. Apart from an unexpected hiccup against a scratch London Counties team, the Springboks had carried all before them. They had recently overcome Wales in a tight game at Cardiff having already thrashed the Irish in Dublin and completely obliterated Scotland in a 44-0 massacre at Murrayfield scoring nine unanswered tries in the process.

John claimed his by now usual place in the middle of the back row where he was joined by Don White and a new cap in Bath's Alec Lewis. Alec was to become a close friend and later played a significant part in John's decision to join the then slightly less prestigious Georgian city club rather than Bristol as might have been expected.

The team now had two new but impressive wingers in his Oxford compatriot Chris Winn and the Wasps burly flier Ted Woodward. John might have been again forgiven for expecting to lead the team but, selectors being selectors, turned back to Richmond's Dr Nim Hall, a man they had summarily axed immediately following John's debut in Dublin back in 1949.

Although John's debut had been just under three years before, only Hall and Lew Cannell had played in that first match in Dublin and were still on the England radar. In fact, both had also experienced lengthy spells out of the side during the intervening period. By contrast, John had been selected for every single match and indeed played in them all apart from his late withdrawal from that game at Swansea the previous season. This said a lot for how he was viewed in spite of the capricious nature of selection committees.

It was a match that swung to and fro. Hennie Muller hit a post with a penalty and it bounced over the crossbar whilst Bill Hook did likewise and it bounced back out again. Chris Winn scored a try which might have been disallowed but the Springboks prevailed at the death and thus claimed a 'Grand Slam' over the four British nations. Indeed, they were to go on to a clean sweep when they defeated the French in Paris.

In his book on the tour the South African rugby writer R. K. Stent commented,

> Often in the picture was Kendall-Carpenter with his splendid covering on defence and leading the forward rushes

but at the end it was South Africa's day.

There was one more confrontation still to come. The Barbarians had agreed to play the 1948 touring Wallabies in an extra match to help defray the touring team's expenses. This venture had proved so successful that a similar match was added to the end of the Springbok tour. With this in mind, several of the provisional Barbarians team – including John – had been brought together for a bit of a warm-up over the Christmas holidays in a match against Leicester.

True to form, whilst John appeared at Leicester in his usual position in the back row (and did likewise in the intervening Internationals with the 'Boks and Wales), when he ran out in front of a full house at the Arms Park he was once again required to prop with Neath's Rees Stephens taking over his normal place in the middle of the back row.

In what was described in Nigel Starmer-Smith's Barbarians history book as a 'rather error-strewn match', the Springboks rounded off their tour comfortably with a 17-3 victory. Although they only out-scored the Ba-Bas by two tries to one there was never much doubt as to the final outcome.

So ended John's battles with the men of South Africa.

12

Becoming 'Sir'

Clifton College, so named by being situated in the Clifton district of Bristol, was founded in 1862 and had an enviable tradition of both academic and sporting excellence. Unusually for the public schools of the Victorian era it placed an emphasis upon science rather than merely confining itself to the usual unremitting diet of Latin and Greek.

According to Harry Barstow, in his comprehensive history of Bath RFC, Clifton's rugby pedigree went back to the middle of the nineteenth century and it was apparently not for the faint-hearted.

> Having been founded barely two years previously in 1862, Clifton College nonetheless embraced rugby football almost as soon as the school opened its elegant front door to their first intake of pupils.

Barstow then goes on to describe the earliest known inter-school match ever to be held in England when Clifton travelled, courtesy of Brunel's recently completed West Country railways, to play Marlborough. One problem at that time was that the formation of the RFU was still a decade into the future and each school played to its own set of rules. Those rules generally allowed not only tackling but also tripping, 'scragging' and something called 'the squash' which somehow sounds particularly nasty. Marlborough however drew the line at hacking whereas Clifton cheerfully encouraged it.

Apparently Clifton started hacking away merrily and after a few futile protests Marlborough began to do the same and things soon began to get out of hand. Barstow then recounts a lovely exchange between Clifton's captain J. A. Boyle and the travelling master in charge Dr Bradley.

> Boyle: I think we'd better stop the game sir, hadn't we?
> Dr Bradley: No, no! They'll think we are afraid of them. Win the game first and then talk about stopping if you like.

No wonder the sun never set upon the British Empire!

This early sporting reputation was also gained at cricket and indeed Gloucestershire doctor W. G. Grace sent his eldest son (also called W. G.) there for his schooling.

In more recent years the heavy blitz on Bristol and Avonmouth during the Second World War had seen the school decamp temporarily to Bude in North Cornwall whereupon the school grounds had been used by both British and American forces as a base. By the time John arrived there in 1951 things had largely returned to something like normality, although many things were still rationed and much of Bristol had been reduced to a rubble-strewn bomb site.

One of Clifton's Old Boys was a fellow Cornishman named Dr Keith Scott who had also recently captained England – in his case in the first peacetime International after the war. John was naturally expected to coach the rugby but was also to discover that the school already had an ex-England rugby forward on its staff in the Revd Peter Brook as the school chaplain having previously served with the Army out in Burma.

As far as other sport at Clifton was concerned, they had a well-known local middleweight boxing champion named Gordon Hazell who took PT and gymnasium work plus a professional cricket coach and various masters who helped to look after the rugby in the autumn term. There was a choice of cross country, hockey, etc. in the spring term and finally the summer was given over to athletics and cricket. John was clearly to be part of all that but his main topic was to be History with a bit of English and Economics thrown in as required.

Whilst John was just starting out on his first job, his fiancée Toby had been working as a matron at a prep school at Seaford in her home area of East Sussex. It was already six years since they first met but John had first to attain his degree and then have a house and a regular source of income before any serious thoughts of marriage and starting a family could be contemplated. Indeed, when he first arrived at the school, he was naturally only a Junior Master and was assigned to Dakyn's House. This still only warranted his living in an assigned room rather than enjoying the vital provision of accommodation for a family. He would need to become responsible as a full House Master in order to attain this as part of an employment contract which would at last make marriage feasible.

With his Fleet Air Arm background, he was also soon heavily engaged with the school's combined cadet force. In those days of much larger armed services and a mandatory period of National Service it made perfect sense for the more affluent independent schools to provide this and it gave pupils a head start to soon becoming officers when they were to be 'called up'.

Clifton also had a reputation for developing young men to maximise their own particular talents. During John's time at the school two very different characters serve as examples of this. One was David Perry who went on to emulate many of John's exploits on the rugby field, earning his University Blue – in his case with Cambridge – and then going on to captain England from the Number 8 position in the mid-1960s much as John had done just over a decade earlier.

Another was John Cleese, the comic actor, whose exploits in Monty Python, as Basil Fawlty and in several major movies make him arguably one of the most famous of all Clifton's 'Old Boys'. He was already well over 6 feet tall when he arrived and as such might have been marked out as a potential second row forward. However, rugby just wasn't really his 'thing' although he apparently was a more than useful bowler in the cricket team. John was actually Cleese's 2nd XI cricket coach and was quite a decent cricketer in his own right who might have been even better had he been encouraged to bat and bowl left-handed which was his naturally stronger side.

Cleese was also already known for thinking up some outlandish pranks such as placing a tailor's dummy on the school roof and painting some footsteps down from the statue of Field Marshal Haig (another very different famous alumnus) to the nearest boys' toilet and then back again onto its plinth.

An ambitious man like John was never going to stay as a Junior Master very long and the next logical step was going to be that promotion to House Master and thus acquiring that all-important family accommodation. Going hand in glove with this would be getting married and then probably giving up playing rugby. Before too long he was to take over East Town House which was for the first time specifically set up for day pupils – like John Cleese – from the immediate Bristol area. Times change and the school now has no fewer than six such houses of which three are for girls.

A few of John's former pupils recalled him as a tall, upright figure invariably dressed in a sports jacket. All teachers get nicknames which can often be either slightly cruel or rather obscure. John's moniker was neither; he was generally just referred to as 'KC'. As far as possible he left much of the discipline to be meted out by the house prefects, only intervening by exception in more serious situations. When he did so he tended to avoid corporal punishment, preferring to think up rather bizarre forms of retribution which he continued when he later became a headmaster. One of his former pupils (at another of his schools) described being forced to sit on the grass in front of the school for a couple of hours transferring water from one bucket to another with a spoon.

You would hardly ever find a modern rugby player smoking but back in the 1950s virtually everybody did so and he was no exception. Pupils would go to see him in his study to find themselves peering through a thick fog of tobacco smoke despite the fact that he invariably used to stub out his cigarette and open a window as soon as they arrived. When he moved to Kent as a headmaster in 1961, he quickly gave it up – partly because he wanted to set an example in a school where pupils caught smoking would get into serious trouble and also because the medical profession were just beginning to issue dire warnings about the links between smoking and lung cancer.

Another thing which pupils noticed rapidly was that, although he affected to appear laid-back, he was actually already quite a driven individual and had already developed the habit of working long into the night. Whilst he was only a Junior Master, he was self-evidently extremely ambitious. Not for nothing had he led both his university and his country on the rugby field and he was clearly bound for 'higher things'. But where?

He had already turned his back on any thoughts of the Stock Exchange but perhaps politics, the diplomatic service or being the head of his own school were possibilities at the time. In due course he was going to get more than a taste of all of them.

Among John's cuttings and memorabilia are several fliers for a young Anthony Wedgwood-Benn who had only recently taken his seat in the House of Commons for the first time as the member for Bristol South East. He was exactly the same age as John, both had seen service as fliers in the RAF and the Fleet Air Arm respectively and at that early stage Benn was a lot less left-wing than he subsequently became. According to his sons, John never discussed politics with them and felt he was, if anything, 'mildly conservative'. However, another of John's Oxford acquaintances was Shirley Williams among a host of other left-leaning undergraduates of the time. When she later became Minister for Education and he was a leading light in the Headmasters Conference their professional paths were due to cross once again.

As for diplomacy and a working knowledge of the various financial institutions, he was certainly going to need plenty of those when it came to launching a Rugby World Cup. By the bucketload.

A young sea cadet.

The handsome England debutant.

In an Oxford shirt.

Early days with the Pirates. John is the fourth standing player from the right. Sitting to the right on the ground is Harvey Richards, his lifelong friend.

One of three Penzance boys in England colours in 1950. The others are schoolboy internationals Gerald Luke and Jim Matthews.

Above: On the ball in Dublin.

Left: Future wife Iris Anson, always to be known as 'Toby'.

Leading out Cornwall at Redruth followed by a young Bonzo Johns.

Hooker Steeds breaks for England at Twickenham with John and lock Johnny Matthews in support.

Opening the new stand in Penzance, April 1953.

Right: Wedding day in Sussex in 1955.

Below: Being made a bard at the Cornish Gorsedd.

All dressed up for a
CBE from the Queen at
Buckingham Palace.

Above: Opening the 1987 World Cup in
New Zealand. The speech overshot the
allotted time and aborted the TV adverts.

Left: Presenting a model of a Cornish
mine to the new RFU President Ron
Jacobs.

13

A Balancing Act

When he first arrived at Clifton, he was still only twenty-six and approaching the height of his rugby powers. No longer was he a university student who could fit studies and essays around playing and training but he had been assured upon his appointment that he could continue to get the time off to play at weekends. Despite this it would be unlikely that any more lengthy foreign tours would be on the agenda.

Since returning from South Africa, he had picked his matches with a certain degree of care. Following the South West Counties match against the Springboks he turned out the following week for Cornwall against Berkshire at Redruth and scored twice in a comfortable victory. This was followed by another Cornish victory over Devon at Exeter and two more matches against Gloucestershire and Somerset, both of which ended in scoreless draws. The Somerset match took place in the unlikely venue of Wellington, that small town close to the Devon border which he was not then to know was to play such a major part in the latter stages of his life.

In that first term at Clifton, he played no club rugby whatsoever. Apart from the Stanley's match against his old university he kept himself fresh for leading the 'Probables' in the first Trial at Leicester. This hurdle was overcome but the second held at Twickenham turned out to be a bit of a banana skin when The Rest XV once again overturned the putative England XV (with John leading them). John retained his place in the team but the selectors took away his England captaincy and passed it over to the returning Nim Hall.

His club affiliation at the time was still entirely with his home town club in Penzance (although he did briefly turn out for Richmond in a defeat at Gloucester) but it was geographically much too far away from his school duties to be a practical proposition in term time. He realised that if he was going to continue to play for his country, he would need to be playing regular first-class club rugby and that would inevitably mean finding a team nearer to his place of work.

In the meantime, he made a try-scoring return to the Pirates against local rivals St Ives just before Christmas and again at Redruth immediately afterwards.

Despite their remote location, the Pirates were building up an impressive fixture list and in mid-February he returned to line up against the Harlequins, although he was unable to make it back to Cornwall for the visit of Llanelli a fortnight later. He later made further appearances against Cardiff and the Saracens during his school's Easter holidays.

The Five Nations was something not to be missed and the hierarchy at Clifton were no doubt delighted that their new recruit was still very much in the public eye. In those days there were no squad sessions. International teams only gathered for that gentle run out on the Friday afternoon before a match, so an England game at Twickenham would simply entail his taking the train up to Paddington early on a Friday and coming back on the Sunday, thereby only missing a few lessons on the Friday and Saturday morning.

In the wake of the narrow loss to the Springboks, England looked to field an unchanged team for the visit of the Welsh to Twickenham two weeks later. That afternoon session runout, which was rather like the modern-day 'captains run', cannot have been that gentle as it resulted in the late withdrawal of prop Wally Holmes with an injured back. This allowed one of those fearsome Woodgate twins – Eddie – to win his only cap alongside the established duo of Bob Stirling and hooker Eric Evans. Wales had suffered a similar setback when their star centre Bleddyn Williams also had to cry off on the morning of the match.

Another huge crowd descended upon Twickenham and with 73,000 packed into the stadium there were reputedly another 10,000 locked outside. Early on, the brilliant Lewis Jones pulled a thigh muscle but, with no substitutions allowed, had to limp through the match in the accepted – if medically insane – practice of the time. It was a thrilling if rather disjointed match with several injuries and many stoppages but the Welsh backs, despite the handicap to Lewis Jones, were far superior to their English hosts.

Each side scored two tries but a single conversion by Malcolm Thomas led to a final score of 8-6 in favour of Wales. John played a major role in the build-up to England's second by the hefty Wasps winger Ted Woodward. England might well have snatched the match in the dying seconds when John's friend and later Bath teammate Alec Lewis dived over the try line only to be recalled by the Irish referee for a forward pass. England had played much better than the previous season but still had lost both their matches, albeit by very small margins.

All this would have caused great excitement with the boys back at Clifton. Compared with today sports coverage at the time was very sparse. Hardly anyone outside of a few wealthy people in London had television sets – although this was to change dramatically the following year in time for the Coronation – and the BBC was the only TV channel in the country. Rugby was very rarely shown and often the best way to see some very stilted highlights of an England match was to go to the cinema a few days later and see it on Pathe or Movietone newsreels. These would be screened for about ten minutes between the main feature and those advertisements for supposedly 'healthy' untipped cigarettes, Morris Minor cars and apparently miraculous washing powders.

Newspaper coverage was however fairly comprehensive and very fast. A large provincial city like Bristol could produce and distribute its Saturday evening '*Green Un*' or '*Pink Un*' (depending upon where you were) with full reports on not only Bristol City or Bristol Rovers but also all the major rugby and football matches throughout the land as well as results of all the minor league matches taking place locally. Furthermore, they would be for sale out on the streets well before six o'clock. How this was all achieved half a century before mobile phones, the internet, laser printing, etc. is still a matter of wonder.

Finally, of course, there was the good old steam radio. The Beeb did a pretty decent job in this regard with the seemingly omnipresent Irishman Eamonn Andrews hosting Sports Report at 5 o'clock each Saturday evening on what was then known as the Light Programme (an approximate equivalent to Radio 2). Although most of this inevitably centred upon football it included regular broadcasts of boxing, horse racing and, to a certain extent, rugby. The biggest radio winner was Test Match cricket which had been given extensive ball-by-ball coverage since before the war.

Today a radio commentator is usually accompanied by an 'expert summariser' who is usually a retired player earning a modest cheque for giving his or her views on the progress of the match. In those days there was instead a disembodied voice which could be heard rather soberly intoning a number like 'Six' or 'Eleven' as the commentator rattled away doing his stuff. A listener would then need to refer to his copy of the *Radio Times* which would show a diagram of a rugby pitch divided into squares each with its own individual number. From this the listener could hopefully deduce in which segment of the pitch the action was taking place. This innovation had first been introduced for Association Football by the BBC for an FA Cup Final in the late 1920s and somehow survived for another thirty years for both sports until most International and Varsity matches became televised.

On 6 February 1952 – just three days before Ireland were due to play at Twickenham – the King died in his sleep at Sandringham and the country was plunged into deep mourning. By one of those odd historical co-incidences his father (George V) had also died at the same place almost exactly sixteen years earlier just before England had met the Irish in Dublin. Back then Ireland was already a Republic and, although both teams wore black armbands out of respect, his death had occurred over two weeks before the match and the game had gone ahead. This time the match was postponed for a month.

With the trip to Paris not scheduled until April, John's next cap was therefore to be gained up at Murrayfield against the Scots. Apart from restoring Wally Holmes, the selectors had left the pack intact but had rung further changes behind the scrum. One of these was the omission of Gloucester's Bill Hook at full-back. Hook had been included partly for his prowess as a goal-kicker but had experienced a miserable time with the boot, missing four conversion attempts out of four plus several penalty attempts over the two previous matches and hence paid the price.

John would have been pleased to have seen fellow Cornishman John Collins from Camborne given his chance in Hook's full-back jersey. Scotland had 'enjoyed' a thoroughly dreadful season following on from that 0-44 debacle against the Springboks with three more depressing defeats against France, Wales and Ireland. England fielded the exact team – including Collins – which had been selected to face the Irish five weeks before.

At half-time England led by a mere five points but ran away with the match in the second half to score three more tries. One of these came from John – courtesy of a back row move involving flanker Don White – to finish with a resounding 19-3 victory.

The Irish match finally took place at the end of March but did so in a late winter blizzard which kept the crowd down to only about half the mass of humanity which had poured into Twickenham back in January. England won the match by a single unconverted try to nothing but the star of the show was probably Collins who time and again thwarted the rampaging Irish pack on a bone-hard, icy pitch. It was a day seemingly designed for concerted forward foot rushes which was of course meat and drink to those green-shirted banshees as they drove remorselessly through the slush. The gallant Collins dived repeatedly onto the ball and to the rescue, earning himself a thorough 'shoeing' for his pains. The heavier England pack – with John again much to the fore and doing well in the lineouts – slowly gained mastery and secured a second successive victory.

What a difference a week makes! From a barren and freezing London, the same England team found themselves basking in the Parisian spring sunshine where the large crowd included Field-Marshal Montgomery despite his being much more of a football fan supporting his beloved Portsmouth.

France led at half-time courtesy of an unconverted try by their pin-up boy Pomathios, who then had to retire with a badly pulled muscle, thus leaving only fourteen Frenchmen to try to sustain their lead. England had to thank their experienced skipper Nim Hall whose shrewd tactical kicking repeatedly pinned the French onto defence. He also kicked two fine penalty goals, one of which was a massive 55-yard drop-kick to steal the match. England thus finished the season in a much more respectable position with three wins out of five.

John could look back on a very successful season as he returned to Clifton for the summer term. Now that he was settled, he really needed to find a regular club within easy reach of his place of work, which of course ruled out the Pirates. The most obvious destination was surely Bristol.

14

Bristol or Bath

Alec Ormonde Lewis was a remarkable man in many ways. He was five years older than John and, having left the Royal Masonic School where he had been equally as good at football as he had been at rugby, had joined the Army just before the war. He had then fought bravely at El Alamein, Sicily and in Italy before being wounded by an anti-personnel mine. After a further spell in the political hotspot that was Palestine, he had been demobbed and took a job in Swindon where he began, at the ripe old age of twenty-seven, to play soccer in the colts' team of Swindon Town.

He had also been drawn back to playing a little rugby with Swindon RFC but his job had then taken him to settle in Bath. On arrival, the by then twenty-eight-year-old joined the city club as an unknown but – better late than never – had become a new sensation. Within a couple of years, he had starred for his adopted county of Somerset and then found himself packing down as a flank forward alongside John for England against the Springboks at Twickenham. Furthermore, he had kept his place for the entire season.

Although international rugby players never had a fraction of the time together that they do today, no doubt John and he would have discussed their hopes and ambitions on their trips to Edinburgh and Paris. Whilst Bristol and indeed Clifton RFC were both on John's doorstep, neither club had been doing particularly well recently and Bath had an equally strong fixture list – albeit with a smaller supporter base.

A further nudge in Bath's direction could be attributed to the fact that his centre colleague from Penzance – Mike Terry – had also recently been playing a starring role for them which had included a sparkling hat-trick of tries against the Harlequins. In addition, Bath could also be reached quite easily by train as for some obscure reason John had still not taken a driving test. Not many people would have spent countless hours learning to fly an aeroplane, travelled widely across the world but still not have been able drive a motor car.

The city of Bath with its sweeping Nash-designed, elegant Georgian terraces and Roman spa baths has always been a 'must' for any visitors to Britain who venture outside of London. Its rugby club then occupied exactly the same location as it does today on a large recreational field which was then also a venue for cricket and hockey. It is to be found right in the centre of the city next to the elegant Pulteney Bridge and would still be recognisable to anyone who had known it back in the 1950s despite some recent additions at either end of the pitch. The modern professional club has been somewhat grudgingly allowed to build these by the powerful reactionary forces in the city understandably wishing to preserve its Georgian heritage.

Although they were formed back in 1865 before either Gloucester (1873) or Bristol (1886) and played many of the same opponents, Bath had never boasted quite the same pedigree in terms of producing illustrious England players as their two nearest rivals. In fact, their only famous international player had been the pre-war centre 'Gerry' Gerrard who had since been killed in action in North Africa. Several years later his widow Mollie became president of the club, thus becoming only the second woman at that time to have done so. By an odd co-incidence the first had been a lady named Mavis Lawry back at John's only other club in Penzance.

It was back in Penzance that John began the season playing four matches before the term restarted at Clifton. His old friend from Truro School, Harvey Richards, had recently returned to Cornwall after also qualifying as a schoolteacher at Westminster College in London. Whilst he had been there, he had played regularly at fly-half for both Rosslyn Park and Middlesex where he had been instrumental in providing the ball to John's England colleagues Winn and Boobbyer. Harvey had just been elected as captain of the Pirates for what turned out to be a remarkable 1952-53 season when the club went undefeated until March.

John's first match for them was against an invitation team containing several England players raised by his friend Ginger Williams, and the two can be seen together in one of this book's photographs. Having just raised his own team and brought them all the way down to Cornwall, Williams just could not resist turning out for the Pirates and lining up against them!

Everybody seemed to be getting in on the act with these pickup teams of leading players and John then appeared among a host of Welsh internationals for a side raised by Bleddyn Williams against Exeter. There was a whispered theory at the time that these matches were merely a crafty way for leading players to pick up some generous expenses but nobody sought to dig into this too deeply.

Later in September, partially prompted by Alec Lewis, John took his own invited 'International XV' to play against Bath on a day when he finally agreed to throw in his lot with them. Clubs in those days had no floodlights, no coaching and training was generally limited to running laps of the pitch, a few sprints, some parade ground-type PT and a bit of touch rugby. John made it clear he could hardly ever attend these but could just as easily do all that – and probably quite a lot more – back at his school in Clifton. This was found to be acceptable as things were still relatively relaxed and had a very long way to go before the great Bath teams of the 1980s and the iron rule of Jack Rowell.

His first match was for the visit of Llanelli for the traditional 'rag doll' match. This was an obscure tradition that dates back into the mists of time when a little rag doll was attached to one of the goalposts and would then be claimed by the winners. Despite all the vast changes brought about in the professional era when Bath played the Scarlets in the European championship quite recently there she still was.

It would have been nice to record that Bath had triumphed and John had crashed over for the winning try to be carried off shoulder high by adoring spectators. Unfortunately, this was just a pipe dream as Bath were soundly thrashed and slumped to their worst defeat of the season, losing 3-25 into the bargain. Perhaps they had some excuse in that the previous weekend the team had been staying down in St Ives and had all been roped in to aid in the rescue of the crew of a small ship being smashed up in a violent offshore autumn storm.

Throughout the autumn John's appearances for Bath were interspersed with playing for Cornwall in the annual West Country four counties league table. He managed to play in all their three fixtures and scored the winning try in a rare Cornish win at Gloucester. His second Bath match was against Bristol – the team which he might so easily have joined and then have been playing on the other side. He again got a try in a match which finished all square.

Mick Hanna was a scrum-half in the Bath team that year. His memory stretched back over nearly seventy years to a couple of amusing incidents when Bath took on the Harlequins in late November at a murky and totally deserted Twickenham with every sound echoing off the cavernous grandstands. Things got off to a rocky start when the Bath players strolled out on the pitch to test the turf and judge the wind only to be told by some Twickenham jobsworth that they were in breach of the rulebook. He was naturally told with some vehemence precisely where he could stick his effing rulebook!

During the match itself John took exception to the fact that the Quins' tall second row Alan Grimsdell had trodden deliberately all over Bath's Irish centre Kevin O'Shaughnessey. A short fight duly broke out between them accompanied by a lot more effing and blinding of which the few chilly spectators could of course hear every syllable in the empty stadium. What made it funny in retrospect was that they were both to become venerable presidents of the Rugby Union – albeit many years later.

During the second half of Bath's season John was often away on England duty or taking part in Trials. On one other occasion he jumped onto an early train from Bristol's Temple Meads station which finally arrived at Redruth just in time to play for Harvey Richards's Pirates in their local derby against the Reds. It was a real local grudge match in front of a huge crowd including reportedly thirty coachloads of Pirates fans coming from Penzance. It ended in a thrilling 6-6 draw, thus ensuring the continuation of the club's unbeaten record. Immediately the match was over, John had a quick shower and then jumped back onto the next train for the four hours' journey back to Bristol. What a modern-day England coach like Steve Borthwick might have made of this sort of thing being wedged in between two International matches hardly bears thinking about.

Generally, his first season at Bath was felt to have been a success, finishing with three tries in eleven appearances despite all his England, Cornwall, Pirates and Barbarians commitments and not playing his first match until early October.

In any event Bath were certainly pleased to have got their man.

15

A Better Year for England

Throughout the six seasons of John's international career England's results could probably best be described as 'mixed'. Over that period Wales tended to perform at a level above the other four nations whereas poor old Scotland generally found themselves lagging some way behind the rest with just the occasional golden day to keep everyone on their toes. England would simply be consistently inconsistent!

The year of 1953 was in many ways a brighter one for the country as a whole with the spectacular coronation of the then twenty-six-year-old Queen Elizabeth and the conquest of Mount Everest. In the world of sport England regained the Ashes at The Oval and two cherished sporting veterans, Gordon Richards and Stanley Matthews, at last won the Derby and an FA Cup winners medal respectively after many years of near misses. Among all this the England rugby team somehow managed to step up a few gears into the bargain.

The selectors had at last begun to turn away from their apparent fixation with Oxbridge Blues and the Harlequins and had started to appreciate, probably for the first time since the war, that some seriously talented club threequarters had become available and several of these hailed from the North. Two of them were the smooth-running fly-half Martin Regan at Liverpool and a multi-gifted Yorkshire centre from Heckmondwike called Jeff Butterfield. Regan's emergence allowed the captain, Nim Hall, to revert to his preferred place at full-back. Soon a midfield combination of Butterfield and Cannell, coupled with the raw power of Ted Woodward outside them on the wing, meant that England's striking power behind the scrum could compare with the very best.

When the Trials began in early December it looked as though John might regain the England captaincy when he led the Whites to a comfortable win over the Colours at the remote rugby outpost of Workington. However, a tame draw in the second at Exeter led the selectors to turn back to Hall for the final one at Twickenham. John's contribution included an unusual try when he caught a 25-yard drop out and burst through a surprised defence to crash over in the corner. Hall might be going to lead the side but there was no way John was going to be left out altogether.

When the team ran out onto the pitch at Cardiff Arms Park it was to be the one and only time John faced the *'hwyl'* and passionate singing of the home crowd. He had already been there a couple of times with the Barbarians, including the face off with the Springboks, but these were relatively sedate affairs compared with an occasion when fifteen red-shirted heroes ran out to do battle against the 'bloody English'.

Due to injuries, Wales were going to have to cope without their star half-backs Rex Willis and Cliff Morgan. Their replacements, Billy Williams and Roy Burnett, had been an admirable pairing for Newport but nevertheless John and his colleagues in the England back row must have rubbed their hands and felt this was going to be a golden opportunity to cause a bit of mayhem.

England prevailed despite their debutant hooker Nick Labuschagne being repeatedly penalised in the set scrums and once again John's defensive covering was very much to the fore. Added to this, Don White gave Burnett a very uncomfortable afternoon forcing him across the field and disrupting the entire Welsh back line. Lew Cannell claimed the only try to be scored that afternoon but England then had to defend for their lives in the last ten minutes but ultimately prevailed to send 56,000 Welshmen home sorely disappointed.

The team travelled across to Dublin in the unusual position of being on the back of four consecutive victories and the only change was to restore the ebullient Eric Evans in place of Labuschagne. It was in many ways the match of the season which England could equally have won or lost during a ding-dong contest. As it turned out to be a 9-9 draw neither side could feel entirely satisfied. Jack Kyle, leading the Irish, repeatedly pinned England back in defence during the first twenty minutes. Once again John and his Bath teammate Alec Lewis earned plaudits in the press for their containment job as they took an increasingly tight grip on both the Irish half-backs Johnny O'Meara and Kyle himself. Hall put over a couple of penalties but, if only he had managed to land a relatively easy conversion of a fine try by Eric Evans, England would have gone on to a Grand Slam.

Next up on the fixture list was the visit of France to Twickenham. By this time John's perennial opponent Guy Basquet had left the international scene to be replaced by the equally talented and long-serving Maurice Celaya from Biarritz. For England's part the third member of the back row trio, Don White, was to be absent through injury. The selectors then turned to an all-action policeman with two unusual Christian names, Dyson Stayt Wilson, although he was universally known as 'Tug'.

Tug was less of a destroyer than White and he was only to play the one international during that particular season. Undaunted, he was to go on to become an ever-present throughout the next couple of years and indeed to then enjoy a highly successful tour with the Lions in South Africa.

France entered the match having had to make several last-minute changes due to injuries and England swept to a comfortable victory by three tries to none. In doing so they introduced Jeff Butterfield for the first time in the centre to partner Cannell. The debutant stole all the headlines by intercepting a wayward

French pass before sending Woodward sailing over for England's first try. He then finished off the match by ghosting over the line himself to send the big Twickenham crowd home happier than they had been for a very long time.

If the French match had given them something to cheer about, the England faithful could hardly believe their eyes when three weeks later Scotland were routed by what was in those days the extraordinary tally of six tries to two. In truth Scotland were going through a particularly dismal period and were without Doug Elliot who was their only forward who could conceivably stand any sort of comparison with John.

England were thus to top the Five Nations championship for the one-and-only time during John's six seasons of international rugby. He still stood out like a beacon in an otherwise workmanlike pack but England could at last boast some real potency in their backs in men like Regan, Woodward, Cannell and now Jeff Butterfield. It was an exciting prospect that the All Blacks were due to visit the following season. Older followers of the game had even begun to dare to dream once again.

Before the season ended there was yet another Barbarians Easter tour to South Wales although this time John appeared at Penarth and Swansea with the tourists winning on both occasions. Before he was due to report back to Clifton for the summer term, he returned to Penzance where he again played a few matches for the Pirates including yet another game in front of a full house against Cardiff.

Since the Pirates had moved to their compact Mennaye Field at the end of the war their facilities had been extremely basic. They lacked both a clubhouse and a grandstand and with just an old converted Nissen hut serving as a changing room. This state of affairs was not for want of ambition – nor even money – but in the immediate post-war era obtaining building materials for anything other than repairing bomb damage was well-nigh impossible. By 1953 things had at long last begun to improve and a modest steel-framed stand capable of housing about 500 spectators had been built largely by local volunteers.

With the coronation imminent this was rather grandly named as the 'Queen Elizabeth Stand' and John was asked to open it. A photograph still hangs proudly in the club's spacious clubhouse (acquired just a couple of years later) showing John alongside various civic dignitaries in sensible shoes and mayoral chains doing the honours before the last match of what had been the club's most successful season in its albeit very short history.

16

Here Come the All Blacks

Ever since the game of rugby became a major sport, the New Zealand rugby team has generally enjoyed the position of being recognised as the World's Number One. From time to time this lofty position has been taken over by South Africa and arguably once or twice by Wales. Nevertheless, after a year or two, those hardy men in their black shirts with the silver fern on their chests invariably rise back to the top by soundly defeating whoever is pitched up against them.

Despite all his achievements and his widely considered reputation as a 'world-class' player, John had never yet taken the field against them. It will be recalled that he might well have done so with the British Lions three years before but the need to obtain his university degree and thus qualify to become a schoolmaster had rendered his going out to New Zealand an impossibility.

Now at last they were coming to Europe to undertake a lengthy tour of the British Isles and France for the first time since 1935 when King George V was still on the throne. Then they had been defeated by England in their very last match in Britain during which England's flying blond Russian winger Prince Obolensky had written himself indelibly into rugby folklore. Hopes had begun to run high that history might somehow repeat itself.

At the end of the war a strong team of New Zealand servicemen who were already serving in Europe – popularly known as the Kiwis – had played a large number of matches around Britain. These had included four unofficial international matches before boarding their ships for the long voyage home. That was now no less than eight years before when John was still just a twenty-year-old rookie beginning to find his feet with the fledgling Pirates down in Penzance.

One of the stars of that Kiwi team had been a brilliant full-back named Bob Scott who had served in North Africa and Italy as a truck driver in the New Zealand army. Now at thirty-two and with very little hair still left on his head, he was returning for his career swansong back in the United Kingdom. He had come through a tough upbringing being one of six children whose own father had been seriously wounded in the First War at Gallipoli. Since returning to New Zealand after that Kiwi tour he had performed wonders both on the All

Blacks' tour to South Africa in 1949 and against the Lions a year later. As with fellow goal-kicking full-backs George Nepia in the 1920s and later Don Clarke in the 1960s, he was destined to be the chief crowd-puller. It was rumoured that as a party trick he could bang over penalty goals from the halfway line in his bare feet.

In looking at the itinerary John would have picked out three potential matches when he might have hoped to play against them. These would have been with England, the Barbarians and another combined Cornwall and Devon team. He would also have noted that the tourists would be led by a back row man named Bob Stuart who was in due course to become a lifelong friend and this continued right up to – and indeed throughout – the fraught days of the inaugural World Cup thirty years later.

Those 1953-54 All Blacks included a number of other particularly fine players including the towering lock forward 'Tiny' White, boxing champion and prop forward Kevin Skinner, Don Clarke's elder brother Ian, flying winger Ron Jarden and fly-halves Vince Bevan and Laurie Haig. Furthermore, as if to demonstrate how rugby talent often runs in families, they boasted a star centre named Brian Fitzpatrick whose son Sean was of course to enjoy a wonderful career of his own as an All Blacks captain in the 1990s.

The season turned out to be John's last one in the England team. The selectors, having finally found a winning captain in Nim Hall, promptly put him out to grass and then turned, not to John, but to the veteran RAF prop forward Bob Stirling. He had made his international debut three years earlier at the ripe old age of thirty-one having risen from the ranks to becoming a wing-commander during the war and been the RAF Heavyweight Champion as a boxer. He had formed a powerful unit with hooker Eric Evans and could be relied upon to tough it out with anyone, but he was hardly likely to possess the tactical nous that John could have brought to the leadership role.

Cornwall however saw things differently and belatedly appointed John as their leader for the first time, a position he was to hold until his final retirement from the game three years later. Under his leadership the county team made a somewhat stuttering start losing narrowly at Penzance to a British Police team and then scraping a single-point victory over a pick-up Dai Gents XV at Redruth. When it came to the important stuff in the County Championship, a highly encouraging victory against Devon – courtesy of another fine try from Mike Terry – was followed by an engrossing draw with a strong Gloucestershire team.

All now depended on a final match with Somerset at Bridgwater. Despite John's very best efforts and encouragement the match ended in a rather unsatisfactory 0-0 draw, thus blowing Cornwall's first real chance of making the semi-finals since the war. There was nevertheless one consolation in that he was now the obvious candidate to lead the South West Counties against the All Blacks a few weeks later.

This was a year when St Luke's College in Exeter were carrying all before them and made the headlines by scoring the remarkable total of over 1,000 points in a season. This of course is not so unusual in modern rugby but one has to remember that a try was then worth only three points, kicks at goal had to be attempted with old rugby balls which got heavy in the wet and there were no kicking tees. Furthermore, being a college, their season did not last as long as that of a normal rugby club.

Rather like Loughborough, St Luke's was a training college for would-be PE teachers and for some years had attracted a host of highly talented Welshmen – and indeed Cornishmen – and this particular team boasted a particularly bumper crop. Perhaps upon reflection selecting only two of them was a mistake, but it was nevertheless a reasonably strong side. Once again, the artificial 'political balance' of picking exactly eight Cornishman and seven Devonians made for some odd combinations. A good example of this would have been Cornwall's talented fly-half Harry Oliver being paired with a Devonport scrum-half named Meadows whom he had never even met before.

On Wednesday 9 December around 18,000 fans poured into the Recreation Ground at Camborne with its gently undulating pitch and a rather ornate old wooden Grandstand which dated back to Edwardian times. The All Blacks had not been having matters all their own way and had just survived with a narrow 3-0 victory at Leicester over the previous weekend. After Camborne they were next to visit Wales where they were destined to record a mere draw with Swansea before losing to the full Welsh national team.

John's future friend and All Blacks' captain Bob Stuart did not manage to make the trip to Cornwall as he was laid up back in London for treatment on an injured knee. In fact, with other players carrying various examples of wear and tear, John's opposing Number 8 was to be the prop forward Ian Clarke who thus was playing well out of position. The tourists suffered a further setback when they lost their big lock Nelson Dalzell to an eye injury but, whilst that all-Cornish back row trio of John, Roberts and Bone were able to cause a fair amount of havoc, the All Blacks ultimately proved to be too strong.

The *Daily Mail* once again paid tribute to John's tireless corner-flagging defence, but the tourists managed nevertheless to come away with a fairly decisive 9-0 victory.

Several years later in an interview with a journalist he ruefully recalled,

I sometimes feel I'd like to be buried in Cornwall and once I nearly was. It was when Cornwall and Devon played the All Blacks during their 1953-54 tour. Their fly-half Laurie Haig had aimed a long diagonal kick from his own half towards touch near the Counties' line. It was my lot to be the only one of the home team able to get back in time to fall on the ball.

I knew my duty. I arrived and cradled the ball to me and had no time to rise before the All-Blacks pack descended. The incident is vivid to this day for, as if I were being picked clean like a chicken carcass, the New Zealanders set about me with almost clinical precision to heel us both back to their scrum half, who, discarding me like a husk, passed the ball swiftly out.

Cornish crowds were invariably vociferous in their support for their heroes and could be quite intimidating at times. Although the game was generally played in an excellent spirit, they took exception to one incident on the field and there was a prolonged storm of loud booing from the packed banks around the pitch.

John promptly marched up to the touchline like the irritated schoolmaster he had by now become and shouted at them to 'Shut up!'. They did.

Clearly it still rankled with him after the match. Later that evening at the post-match dinner in Penzance he rose to his feet for his speech as the home captain and this was duly reported in the *The Cornishman*, the area's local weekly newspaper.

> We don't expect to hear any moaning in a game and, if there is any, we like to feel that it comes not from those on the field but from the crowd. Today we kept that to a minimum.

By this time in his career, he was very much the 'senior prefect' among the playing fraternity and he had developed some strongly held views as to how the game should be played. At times this could frankly make him rather grumpy. On one occasion a Gloucester v Bath match at Kingsholm had become predictably feisty with lots of stray boots and fists flying around and a succession of off-the-ball scuffles breaking out. At one point he marched up to his captain and told him bluntly that he was not enjoying his afternoon and suggested that he call the match off. Given the likely reaction from The Shed had he done so, it was probably just as well that his skipper had the good sense to ignore him.

Sandwiched in between the games for Cornwall, John managed to get away for a handful of games for Bath who were having a mixed season. After an exciting early Autumn match with yet another of those random gatherings of current and recent international players – in this case appearing as Nim Hall's XV – Bath contrived to go down 0-13 to a modest Bridgwater team. As so often happens the lesser club rose to the occasion and soon afterwards Bath only just scraped a draw with Cheltenham.

With England due to play five Internationals that season only two Trials were deemed to be necessary. Possibly with the captaincy in mind (or perhaps because the selectors were undecided whether to keep him in the team at all?) John was asked to lead the 'Possibles' in the first one at Nottingham. They were soundly defeated by the 'Probables' but nevertheless he was reinstated in the England XV when they played out the final trial at Twickenham in the New Year.

By the time the All Blacks came to London at the end of January, they had recovered from their defeat at Cardiff and had since beaten the Irish in Dublin as well as the Midland Counties at Aston Villa's stadium – Villa Park – in Birmingham. By the same token England had defeated Wales for a second year running, so hopes ran high for another stirring victory against their famous visitors.

Accordingly, a full house of 72,000 made their way to Twickenham in an optimistic and perhaps even an expectant mood. England had retained their half-backs Regan and Rimmer with the potency of Butterfield and Woodward and the future Rugby League star Pat Quinn outside them. They also introduced the powerful Phil Davies from the Harlequins who was destined to form a great midfield partnership with Butterfield and Quinn eighteen months later when the Lions toured South Africa. As far as the back row were concerned, Alec Lewis had picked up a frustrating injury playing against Gloucester and, although he was still performing well, perhaps his age was now beginning to play on the minds of the selection panel. Whatever the reason, John and Tug Wilson now had a new recruit packing down beside them in the back row in the person of Reg Higgins who was a tearaway Lancastrian from the Liverpool club.

The pack also included a brand-new second row pairing of a Clifton RFC old boy named Peter Young who had the unusual distinction of being selected whilst he was currently playing his club rugby over in Ireland for Dublin Wanderers. The other lock was a long-standing Wasps stalwart named Peter Yarranton who, like John, was later destined to become president of the Rugby Union, as indeed was a new prop called Sandy Sanders. Sanders had forced his way into the side after having only joined the Harlequins at the beginning of the season with his rugby prior to that being limited to the unlikely colours of Ipswich YMCA.

Bob Stuart was back to lead out New Zealand, who had all their stars like White, Scott, Jarden and Laurie Haig fit and raring to go. It was another bitterly cold day and there was the familiar sight of the touchlines being surrounded by tons of straw which had been laboriously removed from the playing surface. Although most other matches around the country had been called off, somehow this one was able to go ahead.

It was all to end in bitter disappointment. There was only one score in the entire match when, midway through the first half, a foot rush by the All Blacks resulted in new England full-back Ian King diving bravely onto the ball only to be rucked unceremoniously off it (shades of John's recent experience at Camborne). This led to Dalzell, now fully recovered from his injury in Cornwall, crashing over the try line with Bob Scott unerringly adding the conversion.

John and the rest of the pack tried might and main but – apart from a couple of thrilling dashes from the hefty Ted Woodward which briefly brought the crowd to their feet – Stuart's pack took a stranglehold on the play. Furthermore, they never released it and the big crowd were left at the final whistle to ponder yet another of those frustrating 'might-have-beens'.

A final opportunity to have a go at the All Blacks could well have come when they played their penultimate match in the British Isles. In preparation for this match the Barbarians had included John in the pack for what was effectively a practice run-out against Leicester. It had performed brilliantly but perhaps they were flattered by a below-par showing from the Tigers. The upshot of all this was that there was no place for John and whereas Clem Thomas, Sid Judd and Don White were all fine players in their own right, the team sadly missed the lineout contribution and defensive organisation which he might have been able to bring to the party.

The final score of 19-5 to the tourists only tells part of the story. The All Blacks took control in the first half and then let rip in the second and soon it was all over and time for the traditional singing of 'Auld Lang Syne' and 'Now is the Hour'.

Welsh crowds are of course brilliant at this but perhaps they would have sung even louder after a Barbarian win. It would be another twenty years before Gareth Edwards and THAT try would send the bread and arias rising up to a rainy Cardiff heaven.

The next time John was to find himself pitted against a group of aggressive New Zealanders would have to wait another thirty years – and that would be across a conference table.

17

Last Call with England

Apart from the visitors from New Zealand there was also the no small matter of another Five Nations series to be contested. England had finished the previous season on top of the table thanks to three victories and a draw in Dublin. Wales were generally considered to pose the greatest threat every year but they were going through something of a transition. On the other hand, they had just beaten the All Blacks and a few of the old stars such as winger Ken Jones, scrum-half Rex Willis and lineout specialist Roy John were still very much around. Even if the wonderful Lewis Jones had by then decamped to Rugby League there were still men like Cliff Morgan and Sid Judd coming into the side and able to pick up the mantle.

Added to this a new group of highly talented youngsters were waiting in the wings and about to make their mark. These included the two unrelated Merediths. The first was the hooker Bryn who had just played at Camborne alongside John in the combined counties team and the other was Courtney, a skilful and very mobile prop from Neath. Another big man with a very big future was the Llanelli lock Rhys Williams who was destined to become one of the precious few Lions forwards whom both the Springboks and the All Blacks freely admitted that they would have loved to have had playing on their side.

They came to Twickenham as usual in mid-January two weeks before England were due to welcome the All Blacks. It proved to be a bit of a rough and tumble sort of match with lots of mistakes in an unforgiving midwinter wind. For all that it had moments of great excitement, especially when Ted Woodward was given the ball and made storming dashes down the right wing scattering red shirts before him like chaff. One of these shirts belonged to full-back Gerwyn Williams who suffered a dislocated shoulder in trying vainly to stop one of the bullock-like Woodward's two tries.

John had gone through a relatively quiet match by his standards, although he did have a hand – or rather a foot – in England's winning try in the dying seconds of the game. During a late England attack and with the match tied up at six points apiece, a pass to John went to his ankles and, unable to catch it, he nevertheless managed to get a boot to it, steering the ball into the path of winger Chris Winn who followed up and dived on it to claim a breathless victory.

It was in many ways a cruel blow to Wales, who lost their scrum-half early in the second half leaving fly-half Cliff Morgan to work the scrum with a consequent major disruption to their attacking force. As already mentioned, in those days no thought was given to replacements and many a match would be disrupted in this way. For all that Wales so nearly forced a draw.

The All Blacks match came and went and, whilst England had lost, an unchanged team was sent out to play Ireland. It was now a few years since Ireland had won the Grand Slam and their old leader Karl Mullen had by then departed the scene. Worse still was the fact that their talisman and fly-half Jack Kyle had to withdraw before the game, thus missing his only international match in a record-breaking run from 1946 up to 1958.

The Irish included an interesting Number 8 in James Murphy-O'Connor. For those of the Roman Catholic faith his surname may ring a bell, as he was the elder brother of Cardinal Cormac Murphy-O'Connor who became Archbishop of Westminster. James was a long and lean individual with the programme notes declaring him to be 6 feet and nearly 5 inches in height but weighing only 13 stone. He was also notable in that whilst playing for Leinster he was credited with introducing the round-the-corner goal-kicking style which of course is almost universal in today's game.

During the match he was to score Ireland's only points when he successfully thumped over a long-range penalty using this approach only to miss a sitter a few minutes later and then to be taken off with a serious back injury – a regular plague to men with his unusual physique. He was never to be selected for Ireland again, although his back injury must have cleared up as he went on to play for Berkshire and father six children.

It was an entertaining match with England getting three tries courtesy of Butterfield, Regan and Tug Wilson and chalking up a 14-3 victory. The back division had generally performed well but the pack had not managed to dominate the seven remaining Irish forwards and somebody was likely to pay the price. Sure enough, when the team was announced to go to Edinburgh three men were to lose their place. One was the Yorkshire full-back Ian King, a second was Peter Yarranton and the third was none other than John.

The rugby writer in *The Times* was moved to include a short obituary on his international caree.,

> One cannot escape a feeling of regret that so outstanding a man as J.MacG.K.Kendall-Carpenter should at last have to suffer the same fate of all those who lose in mobility and stamina what they have built up in weight and experience.

Ouch!

Just to add to his discomfort, the selectors had replaced him in his Number 8 position with a tall second row man – thus playing somewhat out of position – called Vic Leadbetter who was already living in Scotland and playing his club rugby for Edinburgh Wanderers. He had appeared in the second row for the

'Possibles' in the Trial at Nottingham but had not made it to the second one at Twickenham. There was no question that he was a capable player and that his height would prove useful in the lineouts, but how he was expected to organise a defence like John, who had spent several years perfecting the art, remained a mystery.

The selectors' blushes were saved by a disappointingly feeble Scotland whose dire run of results must have seemed endless to their loyal supporters. England ran out as comfortable winners – thanks to a fine performance from centre Pat Quinn. Ironically Scotland did surprisingly well in the lineouts in no small part to the efforts of their big lock Ewan Fergusson who in later life was to be knighted as Britain's Ambassador in Paris.

Still mulling over that rather hurtful *Times* article, John might have reflected wryly upon Mark Twain's oft-quoted quip regarding 'Reports of my recent death have been grossly exaggerated' when he was recalled immediately for the visit to Paris for the final match of the season. The capricious selectors had obviously thought better of it and moved Leadbetter back to his proper position in the second row and brought back hooker Eric Evans who had missed the Scotland match with an injury.

This time it was indeed a last hurrah with England for John, although he was not to know it at the time and several pundits and journalists would press his claims to further caps throughout the following season. John's friend and Bath teammate Alec Lewis had also been brought back but in truth they had to play second fiddle to the French captain Jean Prat and his fellow Lourdes back row man Henri Domec. France duly won by 11 points to 3, which included a sensational try from a young Andre Boniface who was at the outset of a long and distinguished career.

John finished with a total of twenty-three England caps, which doesn't sound a lot by modern standards but at the time placed him as the sixth highest ever. One has to remember that when he was playing there were only four Internationals a year plus a fifth if there was a major tour coming to our shores. Today England play something like twelve times a year and caps are awarded for replacements even if they are only on the field for the last couple of minutes!

With all those England calls John's club appearances were understandably rather spasmodic. He had managed to play just one game for the Pirates when back at home for a family Christmas and even Bath games were only squeezed in wherever possible. A solitary match against St Mary's Hospital in January was his only appearance until early March when a fine victory was gained at the expense of neighbouring Bristol followed by a defeat at Swansea. Perhaps inspired by his exclusion from matters going on up in Edinburgh he turned in a virtuoso defensive performance that afternoon in a narrow victory over Newbridge.

The Easter holidays at Clifton saw yet another return to Cornwall with a run of five matches culminating in a confrontation with Cardiff in which he was able to renew his close rivalry with Sid Judd – a magnificent player who was destined to die tragically of leukaemia when only thirty years of age.

The season ended with a short three-match tour with Bath to Switzerland and France with matches against junior clubs with the attractive names of St Claude,

Givors and Tour du Pin. All of these were overcome comfortably but, according to the *Bath Chronicle*, when John was collected by a couple of teammates after the first match in Geneva he was not entirely satisfied.

> John was a bit miffed after the game complaining he only got a touch of the ball six times.

Clearly there is no pleasing a perfectionist.

18

A Youthful Elder Statesman

As the new season opened, John was still three weeks away from his twenty-ninth birthday and, as such, could certainly have been considered fit enough to continue international rugby if he so desired. After all he was still two years younger than Alec Lewis had been when Alec had made his England debut. Despite his smoking habit and not being the most assiduous when it came to club training – it was virtually impossible to get to train with Bath anyway due to his school commitments – he was a naturally very fit man. Furthermore, the facilities for some fitness work at Clifton were on tap as and when he needed them.

Added to this, his uncanny ability to 'read' the play during a game saved him a great deal of wasted running and so there was no logical reason for England not to pick him again. The new season had an added incentive in that, at the end of it, the British Lions were due to visit South Africa and it had been rather arbitrarily determined that they would only select players under the age of thirty. John could still have qualified on those grounds and, with his sky-high reputation from the Oxbridge tour still in the minds of the Springbok press and public, he would have been assured of a fine welcome.

This was never going to happen for two important reasons. He had recently been promoted at Clifton to run Town House – that new one to cater for the large number of local Bristol boys who could attend the school without the additional expense of boarding. He would thus need to be on the spot almost 24/7 during term time and could hardly disappear for several months with the Lions. The second was that he and Toby were finally due to be married the following summer and it was time to set up a home and hopefully start a family.

The season opened with a couple of matches for the Pirates in what was left of the school summer holiday. John could do just about anything on a rugby field and for some time journalists had reported upon his unusual gift for a forward of being able to punt a ball for long distances. On the practice field he had recently found himself a new toy – kicking drop goals.

Members of a pack trying to kick drop goals are virtually unheard of in senior rugby during the past couple of decades – only one by New Zealand's

Zinzan Brooke comes readily to mind – and one can only imagine a modern coach having apoplexy if one of his lock forwards tried one on a whim. This of course did not apply back in 1954 and in his first match for the Pirates against Ginger Williams's invitation team he took the ball from a lineout and thumped over a sensational goal from close to the touchline. The large crowd first gasped, then roared and finally broke into laughter mixed in with prolonged cheering.

That happened on a Saturday and just four days later he was back at Bath facing another guest team raised by Alec Lewis when he performed his new 'party piece' once again. The Bath Heritage website described it thus:

> Talking point of the match was John Kendall-Carpenter's gigantic drop goal. It was quite a fantastic piece of work, but exactly what one can expect from the former England captain.

At the end of the month Bath undertook a short tour down to Cornwall playing against Devonport Services, St Ives and the Pirates. Obviously, John would have loved to have been able to join them but the new school year had just commenced at Clifton and his duties now clearly lay back at the school. In fact, Bath lost their match in Penzance and one can only speculate on his reaction when he heard the news.

John was again the skipper of Cornwall and they were to go on to enjoy their best season since the late 1930s. He got back to Cornwall to lead them to victories over the British Police and Dai Gent's XV at Redruth. One interesting facet of the latter match was that his opposite number in the visitors' back row was a young man named Ian Beer who was not only to take over John's place in the England team but also to go on to lead a life with many marked similarities between the two of them. They were both University Blues (in Beer's case at Cambridge) playing in three Varsity matches, both were back row players, both were destined to become headmasters of three different public schools, both played for Bath, both were awarded the CBE by the Queen and both were destined to serve as president of the Rugby Union.

The serious stuff began at Bristol when Cornwall pulled off a breathless 9-8 win over Gloucestershire partially courtesy of a missed penalty from almost in front of the posts by the normally reliable Gordon Cripps. Another interesting footnote was that the opposing full-back, Tom Wells, was by then a colleague of John's on the staff at Clifton. On one occasion Tom caught a high up-and-under with John racing up and bearing down upon him like an avenging angel. Tom neatly sidestepped him to get his clearing kick away and then got a fatherly pat on the head for his achievement. The crowd loved that.

Next up was a rather tense and predictably error-strewn victory over Devon in perfect weather at Camborne which set Cornwall up nicely for a final tilt at the supposed weakest link, which was Somerset. The press reported that at least two England selectors would be coming down to Redruth to watch the match and presumably to run the rule over both John and Vic Roberts who had recently been playing especially well for the Harlequins. In addition, they would have been interested in taking a good look at 'Bonzo' Johns, the beefy young Redruth prop-cum-lock and an exciting talent from Penryn and Loughborough College called Roger Hosen.

The match was a tense one played in a typically Cornish 'mizzle' and in the damp conditions the vital win was secured by a solitary try to nil, and so at long last Cornwall had topped their group. The watching selectors might have had a bit of head scratching to do when they read a very interesting piece on the match by ex-England hooker Harry Toft (himself a previous England selector) writing under the headline 'A Great Forward'.

The whole pack deserves high praise but the outstanding personality was J.Kendall-Carpenter. This player, an independent spirit, baffles his friends from time to time by dawdling his way through a dull game with the detachment of Diogenes, but when his interest is fully aroused, he is truly a great player with two exceptional qualities. He is almost certainly the fastest forward playing today and he knows to a second when to strike.

Two fine runs of his at exactly the right moment first enabled Cornwall to score their winning try and then prevented Somerset from winning what looked to be a certain touchdown. By fast and intelligent covering he alone was able to kick the ball dead in the nick of time.

There you have it and make of it what you will. A modern Coach faced with reams of video analysis might despair at his apparently low 'work rate' but he could still win or save a tight match in a way nobody else could ever hope to emulate. Perhaps that comment of his first captain at the Pirates, Bill Monckton, several years before bears repeating when he spoke of John's 'intelligent idleness' as it was still very much there for all to see.

The first England Trial was to be held at Falmouth back on John's home territory and the selectors had made their call. Roberts, Johns and Hosen were all asked to join the party, as indeed was Tom Wells but, rather like Cinderella, the ball was going to go ahead without John. Aside from his exploits with Cornwall, he had also had a few games for Bath in which he had excelled notably against the Quins and the United Services who were still a powerful team at that time and his case for inclusion was becoming overwhelming. But it was not to be.

One old basic skill that modern rugby players never contemplate is that of the art of dribbling. In John's generation young schoolboys would be taught how to control an awkwardly shaped rugby ball by gently rolling it forward between the insteps of both feet. This could be highly effective when the old, heavy leather balls became difficult to handle, particularly when caked in mud and rain.

When it became a combined effort with an entire pack sweeping forward in unison it had virtually all the power of a present-day rolling maul and crowds used to love it. Perhaps because of their attachment to football the Scots were generally considered to be the past masters at it. Elderly Scots will still recall wistfully the raucous cries of "Feet! Feet!" rolling down the open banks of Murrayfield as half-a-dozen wild-eyed and square-jawed Jocks ploughed through the mud with the ball seemingly glued to their leather-studded boots. It could be like something straight out of that old movie *Braveheart* and any defender who dared to drop on the ball in front of that lot probably deserved the Victoria Cross.

Thus, on a muddy Boxing Day at Leicester John celebrated his final match for the Barbarians when he and England's new flanker Peter Ryan dribbled half the length of pitch in front of the Crombie Terrace to send Ryan over for a try which gave even the 20,000 loyal Tigers' fans something special to cheer.

Two further Trials took place following the one at Falmouth but still John was deemed surplus to England's requirements. The press were both bewildered and perhaps even angry on his behalf. Following the Leicester match the author and columnist Hylton Cleaver, who wrote about every sport from rowing to show jumping, baldly stated that,

The best forward on the field was Kendall-Carpenter. Moreover, his height and toughness make him just the man to stand up to the Welsh pack.

South West reporter John Curnow carried the headline, 'Why leave out Carps is the big rugby puzzle!'

Meanwhile journalist Peter Laker in the *Daily Mirror* was even more outspoken, leading an angry column piece headed 'THIS WOULD BE MADNESS!'

Predictably the selectors took no notice whatsoever and the team to face Wales was announced with John's familiar long double-barrelled name nowhere to be seen.

The team which ran out at Cardiff for the first England match since his removal was for a game that had been delayed for a week due to the weather. It resulted in a 0-3 loss with a single Welsh penalty being the only score. John's direct replacement in the middle of the back row was a big, strong, no-nonsense forward named Phil Taylor who had a long and successful career with Northampton. He was not the quickest but was probably more prepared than John to get in and 'mix it' in all the close exchanges. One way or another no fewer than seventeen penalties were given against England that afternoon and it was poor Taylor who was the unlucky one when he was caught offside right in front of the England posts to concede the only score in a very messy match.

There was something of an additional irony about the situation because there were over 56,000 noisy Welshmen crammed into Cardiff Arms Park. Meanwhile at that very same moment about a hundred miles or so away, John was tearing about in a Bath shirt on a cold and windy pitch in Teddington. This was in front of an estimated forty hardy souls plus a couple of stray dogs in a virtually meaningless game with St Mary's Hospital.

The excitements were nevertheless not all over. Under his leadership Cornwall had coasted past Berkshire in the quarter-finals at Redruth. In a 17-9-win, John had opened the scoring himself when he broke away, chipped the ball past the Berkshire full-back and in the words of Vivian Jenkins in the *Sunday Times*,

followed up at express speed to touch down near the posts.

The Cornish were now destined to play a home semi-final on the same ground against Middlesex. It was the first time Cornwall had reached that far for many a year and over 15,000 arrived at Redruth to cheer on the men in black and gold, hopefully towards the promised land of winning a County Championship. This they had only ever won on a single previous occasion and that was way back in 1908. By 1955 there were still plenty of men and women around Cornwall who remembered that occasion fondly but, even then, it was still a hell of a long time ago.

It must be recalled that in those days, and indeed up until the mid-1980s, the County Championship was a much-prized competition in the English rugby calendar and down in Cornwall it was something of a tribalist obsession. Every year men and women of all ages and backgrounds hoped against hope that this somehow would be THEIR year. Time after time they would have their hopes raised and reach a Semi-final or even a Final only to see their dreams shattered seemingly at the hand of a malevolent fate. If all this sounds a little bit melodramatic you can rest assured that is precisely how it felt.

When Middlesex announced their team a number of faces would have been immediately familiar to John from his England exploits. These included Nim Hall who, unlike John, had been given another final shot in the England team, Ted Woodward, Nick Labuschagne and Peter Yarranton. The focus of attention was nevertheless going to be England's brand-new half-back combination of Doug Baker and the lightning-quick Johnny Williams at scrum-half. This exciting pairing were actually playing their club rugby for their respective school Old Boys teams which even back then was unusual. They consistently performed so well that they joined the Lions party to tour South Africa that summer. Their forthcoming battle with that famed Cornish back row of John himself plus Tony Bone and Vic Roberts was a fascinating prospect and this would ultimately decide the match. For their part the visitors' line-up included no fewer than nine current or future England players, plus two Irish and one Scottish international.

Who would come out on top? It was a stern battle fought out in the early spring sunshine and the noisy Cornish crowd soon got their answer. It was not the one they wanted! Cornwall had somehow managed to contain the threat of Woodward but the match was finally settled by a searing break from Johnny Williams followed by a sublime reverse pass to Doug Baker which caught the entire Cornish team flat footed for the fly-half to sail over the line virtually unopposed. This effectively sealed the locals' fate and the match finished with a 10-3 victory for Middlesex. Thousands of sad-faced Cornishmen trooped out into the grey streets of Redruth silently nursing their disappointment having arrived full of hope and song a mere couple of hours or so before.

John's long-time collaborator Vic Roberts was hailed as Cornwall's best player on the day and he was to go on to enjoy a further opportunity three years later when Cornwall were to make it all the way to a Final at Coventry. In John's case he never got the chance to make another bid for the title. Cornwall were to make a few more unsuccessful tilts at the title before finally being crowned Champions in front of a black and gold tidal wave when over 50,000 crazy Cornishmen packed into Twickenham in 1991.

By that time John was sadly no longer with us as he would surely have relished the occasion.

No, he wouldn't – he would have bloody LOVED it!

19

A Great Performer's Final Curtain

That semi-final match at Redruth was probably the last big match in John's playing career but there was still more rugby to come. He immediately returned to Bath and played a major role in significant victories over Swansea and Neath. He also 'enjoyed' a rare old battle in the lineouts with his direct opponent Bert McDonald where their 'apparent mutual antipathy' livened up an otherwise rather dull match at Bristol.

He had recently accepted the captaincy of Bath and, with his impending marriage now only a few weeks away, it was unlikely that he would be hot-footing it back to Penzance very much in the future. He was to score his last try for the Pirates in a drawn game in early April with Aldershot Services and two days later played another match for them against the check-shirted London Hospital and that finally turned out to be it.

There had been some speculation in the media over the past few months as to just why John had been so summarily jettisoned from even consideration for the England team. Just before England's second match in Dublin Pat Marshall did a piece in his regular *Daily Express* column headed 'Carpenter Goes on Scrap Heap' which may give something of a clue:

Two Welsh forwards told me after the match that if John Kendall-Carpenter had been leading your pack it might have been a very different story.

He went on to speculate,

Certainly, Carpenter is an outspoken man who does not use honeyed words either to selectors or the pack he leads. But surely that is the sort of character an international side needs, the type who should be chosen on playing ability and not whether he is a 'Yes' man.

This may have been very close to the mark. There is no question that John was a highly intelligent man who had thought deeply about the game with an enviable vocabulary encompassing both the erudite and the profane. As we have seen, rugby football in the middle of the twentieth century was administered very much with an 'officers and other ranks' mentality whereby the officials and selectors enjoyed first-class accommodation, liberal if not lavish entertaining and were beholden to nobody. Players on the other hand were given second or even third-class train tickets, miniscule expenses and even expected to provide much of their own playing kit.

To be fair to them the selectors and committee men had all been ex-players, had lived through at least one – if not two – World Wars and had been brought up in an era where an officer's word was always to be accepted unquestioningly. There is a temptation to think in terms of Ludendorff's oft-quoted remark about 'Lions being led by donkeys' but this would be a gross oversimplification. The selectors were clearly decent men with the good of the game embedded deeply into their hearts but they bridled instinctively at any criticism be it from the press, the public and certainly from mere players.

We shall never know whether John gave vent with a few pungent views in a late-night bar on some occasion or other and whether some delicate souls had taken umbrage. In recent years leading sportsmen and women frequently get themselves into hot water with the authorities for some aside on television (viz Will Carling's 'old farts' remark), newspaper columns or, more frequently, on social media platforms like Twitter. Nothing remotely like that existed in John's time and there do not appear to be any particularly inflammatory quotes in any newspaper cuttings that have survived.

Several years later another highly regarded West Country England Number 8, Dave Rollitt of Bristol, was reportedly shunned by the selectors for several years after allegedly letting rip after a particularly inept England performance in Cardiff, and there have undoubtedly been many others.

That long, hot summer of 1955 saw two important events take place. Firstly, the British Lions went out to South Africa and tied the four Test series 2-2 whilst playing sparkling rugby to the delight of huge and appreciative audiences. The squad contained two of John's final England back row colleagues in Tug Wilson and Reg Higgins but no doubt they would have welcomed their talisman from Bath to have been out there with them as well. Apart from anything else he would have been the only one in the party with extensive experience of actually playing in South Africa but then when it came to rugby selection simple logic often seemed to take a back seat.

In truth John had another and more important date in his diary. He and Toby were to be married. Just a week after having played his last match for the Pirates they celebrated their wedding in the parish church in Alfriston, which is a pretty little Sussex village very close to Toby's home and work at Seaford. Ralph Green, who was John's old friend and scrum-half from his Oxford days, did the honours as Best Man.

Then after a brief honeymoon, she went back with him to begin the life of a House Master's wife at Clifton. The role can often be a taxing one as it frequently involves being something of a surrogate mother to small boys away from their families at a boarding school and her prior work with her school in Seaford would have prepared her well for that aspect of her job. In their case the pupils were all day boys with their own families close at hand and, as such, she did not need to be quite so involved as she might otherwise have been. In any event she was soon to have her hands very full as the following year their eldest son, Tim, was born, followed closely by Nick just a year later.

John had accepted not only the captaincy of Bath but he was also to lead Cornwall once again. The role of a county captain or even that at a club was never going to be quite as all-consuming as performing the role at a university. Both teams had experienced committees in place to take care of just about everything other than what actually occurred out on the pitch. Despite this, in a club situation a captain would be expected to have a say in team selection and would normally take a leading role in training. Having a demanding job, such as taking on the full role of a House Master – and now with a wife to consider – was not going to make this easy.

Bath would start training at the beginning of August but most of this would still consist of that dreary diet of road running, lapping a pitch followed by a taxing bout of physical jerks. They might then get into a few lineout drills or do some scrummaging and tackling practice and finish up with some touch rugby. In Cornwall's case, apart from a brief runout before the match, there would be very little preparation whatsoever. Consequently, he could – at a pinch – perform both roles.

On the field he was unquestionably the 'man in charge'. Peter Michell, who though much younger played with John for both the Pirates and Cornwall, said that he and some of the other newer players felt almost obliged to address him as 'Sir', although it is highly unlikely that John would have either expected or wanted that in the least. Michell also gave yet another insight into John's remarkable ability to undertake several unrelated things all at once.

He recalled an occasion at a hotel in Bridgwater the morning after a Cornwall match with Somerset which was followed by a fairly raucous evening afterwards. When John failed to appear for breakfast, Peter as the new boy was sent up to his bedroom to check whether the captain was sleeping off the effects of the night before. Having tapped nervously on the door and tip-toed in, he was amazed to see John sitting up in bed surrounded by a pile of exercise books marking history essays. In fact, that was quite normal for John, who it is rumoured had even taken some pupils' books to mark on his honeymoon!

On the field he continued to be a demanding captain and certainly did not suffer fools gladly. On one occasion in another county match back at Bridgwater a rather soft try was given away largely due to a youthful flanker named Terry Thomas being caught badly out of position. John promptly gave him a loud and spicy roasting which clearly frightened the young man out of his wits. A minute or so later John caught a clearing kick in his own twenty-five and galloped up the field almost to the try line. He realised that he was about to be tackled by a defending winger racing across and so, looking to his left, saw Thomas running like a terrified rabbit outside him to receive a perfect pass and swoop over for the decisive try of the match. Nobody quite knew whether to cheer or just to laugh. For quite a while afterwards he was nicknamed 'Three all Thomas'.

Any hopes of a repeat of the previous season's passage into the knock-out stages disappeared in a puff of smoke with a heavy defeat at the hands of Devon at Devonport. Then, just three weeks later, he was to play his very last match in Cornwall when he signed off with a try when leading the county to a fine 14-6 win over Gloucestershire at Redruth.

As for the season at Bath, it was one of mixed results with the team winning only seventeen of the thirty-eight matches played. John naturally made himself available whenever he could (despite twice suffering a badly broken nose which kept him out for two months in the middle of the season) and was frequently among the try scorers. His final match of any substance was back on the Recreation Ground where he bowed out by scoring yet another try as Bath went down 8-23 to a lively Moseley team.

He had picked up his fair share of injuries along the way including broken teeth and jaw, shoulder and rib injuries and all the usual strains, twists, bruises, cuts and stitches which are part and parcel of every rugby player's life. The thing which was to plague him the most as he advanced into middle age was severe arthritis in both his hips and by the time he was in his mid-thirties he had already begun to walk with a limp. Unfortunately, hip replacement surgery, although by then available, was not yet recommended for those still in their forties and so he had to soldier on in considerable pain until his mid-fifties before he had a replacement operation on both hips.

So ended a remarkable playing career when he was still only thirty and in different circumstances might have carried on for another couple of years. He had already come a very long way from that little boy with the high-pitched voice who had played the female parts in Shakespeare to the man who was widely acclaimed as the 'most knowledgeable man in the game'.

20

A School of His Own

The newlyweds began to settle into their life together at Clifton and soon began to raise a family. Their first son, whom they named Tim – perhaps with a nod to one of his grandfather's many nicknames – was born in 1956 to be followed by Nick just over a year later. As we have seen, John's House was exclusively populated by day boys and thus Toby's experience as a school matron plus stand-in mother that she had gained at Seaford was not called upon as much as perhaps she had expected. In fact, it was probably just as well as very soon she had those two small sons to look after. All that was to change when they got to Cranbrook, when her skills were soon in heavy demand once again.

The end of his distinguished playing career meant that John could now concentrate fully upon his chosen profession. For a man who was nothing if not highly ambitious, this was going to involve far more than pottering along as a Housemaster at Clifton. It was not very long before he had set his course upon running a school himself and putting a host of accumulated ideas into practice.

Although he was still only in his early thirties it was not uncommon at the time for young ambitious men to take charge of an established independent school and he undoubtedly had much to offer. Apart from his fame as a rugby player, he could also point to an Oxford degree, a period of wartime duty in the Fleet Air Arm and a well-documented track record of leadership and man management with Bath, Oxford, Cornwall and of course the England team itself.

As for geographical location, neither he nor Toby had any deep ties to the Bristol area and, whereas Cornwall had only one significant independent school which was of course his old *alma mater* at Truro, the South East encompassing both Kent and Sussex offered a host of possibilities. This was very much home territory for Toby who, as with any young mother, would welcome being closer to her own friends and family. In 1960 the couple had added two daughters whom they named Diana and Elspeth to the growing family and by now it was surely just a matter of time before the right opportunity came up. The following year this indeed came to pass.

Back in Penzance a young talented three-quarter named Jimmy Glover was accepted to begin his own teaching career at Clifton. If his name sounds slightly familiar his daughter Helen Glover was many years later to become a famous Olympic rowing champion. Like John, Jimmy had recently captained Oxford University, played for the Pirates and Cornwall and the prospect of joining his famous neighbour was certainly enticing. However, by the time he reported for duty in the autumn of 1961 John and his family had moved on.

Cranbrook is a small market town in the southern part of Kent not far from Tunbridge Wells and was probably no more than an easy one hour's drive to Toby's home territory. Cranbrook School was what was known as a 'Voluntary Aided Grammar School' and traces its roots back to 1574 when it was granted a charter by Queen Elizabeth. Today it is slightly unusual in that it has the status of being a co-educational state-funded boarding school but when John and his family arrived there to take up the reins in 1961 it was still catering for boys only.

The school had lived under the same headmaster since 1929 and, upon his retirement, his chosen successor had suddenly been taken ill and in fact sadly died within just a few weeks of taking over his post. Thus, the school urgently needed a new face and in all probability someone with a youthful outlook and plenty of new ideas. By 1961, John was thirty-five years of age and would have appealed to many different Boards of Governors. He would be viewed as a potentially thrustful young mind with modern 1960s type attitudes to become the catalyst for change which schools like Cranbrook were undoubtedly going to need. In this specific case it would have done his cause no harm in that one of their most influential governors was the BBC rugby and cricket commentator Peter West who quite possibly encouraged him to apply in the first place.

Peter West's name will crop up again in John's story as Peter was later to chair a sports marketing company named West Nally who were to take on the task of bringing sponsors and television rights to the initial Rugby World Cup in 1987. It must surely be more than a mere coincidence that Cranbrook was to produce two more famous sports – in their case football – commentators in the late Brian Moore of ITV and Barry Davies of the BBC.

Once he had arrived and settled in, John was to prove to be very much the reforming headmaster rather than the still youthful sporting hero. Since his university days, he had not been a particularly diligent trainer but had still retained much of his athleticism and during his latter time at Clifton had once taken on the school 100 yards sprint champion and beaten him. However, during his time at Cranbrook, he began to suffer from that arthritis in his hips which was destined to plague him for the rest of his life.

On being offered and taking the job he made two additional decisions. He took and passed his driving test and then gave up smoking. Of course, Toby had been a driver since her time in the Services and had shouldered the burden of being the family taxi service. His first car was an elderly Hillman Husky which was much later to be followed by a Volkswagen camper van. The first four children had been born when John was at Clifton but the fifth and youngest, whom they christened Giles, came into the world soon after they reached Cranbrook.

A colleague and master named James Bradnock, who became a key and loyal member of John's staff at Cranbrook and later followed him to become a Head of House at Wellington, recalled his somewhat bizarre interview process when they met for the very first time.

> I was met at Staplehurst station by this tall imposing man who bundled me into a rather battered old Hillman which I noticed had some holes in the floor. In the back was a small baby (Giles) in a carrycot and I immediately appreciated the man's ability to do several unconnected things all at the same time. When I arrived, his wife greeted me with a tray of bangers and mash at which point he disappeared for several hours to attend to his multitude of duties with the parting line 'Don't dare talk to her!'

> As I was staying overnight, we finally sat down for an interview at 11.30 at night and I was becoming fascinated by this extraordinary man and immediately felt I could trust his instincts and wanted to work with him.

So began a close working relationship which was to endure for over twenty years.

In his excellent history of the school, another senior master from that time, Peter Allen, described the challenges John faced almost as soon as he stepped through the door. By far the most immediate challenge was that which faced many such schools at the time, simply one of survival.

Independent boarding schools were faced with numerous challenges in the 1960s from all quarters, political, economic and social, and John quickly realised that, in addition to some of the ideas which had formed in his mind whilst a Housemaster at Clifton, there were other unavoidable changes that would have to be made. On arriving in Kent, he soon found himself deeply embroiled in protracted and occasionally acrimonious negotiations with the educational authorities on the continuing status and funding of the school.

In 1964 the country elected a Labour government led by Harold Wilson and they had little sympathy for the perceived elitism of private schools and any new legislation in the field of education was likely to work against establishments like Cranbrook. Indeed, in 1965 the new Education Secretary, Tony Crosland, had declared himself to be a sworn enemy of all forms of selective education both independent and grammar.

Furthermore, many of the boarding pupils were the sons of officers in the armed services posted overseas, members of the diplomatic service or executives working abroad with major British companies. At this time the armed services were being drastically reduced and Commonwealth countries were being granted their independence and no longer welcomed expatriate advisers from Britain telling them how to run their affairs. In other words, the demand for boarding school education was likely to fall rapidly.

One of John's reactions to all this was to champion the idea of opening up schools to girls as well as boys. Many traditional Boards of Governors and headmasters were appalled at the prospect, citing all the obvious objections. In fact, Cranbrook only received its first intake of young girls into their own dedicated Houses at about the time John was to move on. By that time most of the political battles had been fought, minds had been slowly shifted and soon a large proportion of private boarding schools had opened their doors to both sexes. Some others merely closed down and disappeared.

In outlook John probably benefitted from his slightly unusual background. In a country still steeped in a rigid class structure he came from a family and a town which knew at first hand what being a 'have not' actually felt like. Conversely, he had lived out his adolescent and adult life surrounded by high achievers in the armed services, university and of course in the still largely middle-class sport of rugby. Although hailing from the depths of Cornwall, he spoke the received Queen's English and his education ensured he could communicate both verbally and in writing at a very high level.

Indeed, he had already become a prodigious letter writer. One of his first projects was to build a swimming pool for the school and he had begged and pleaded for the funds from parents and ex-pupils. This was so successful that nearly 500 people responded with enough money to not only construct the pool itself but also to heat it and build changing rooms as well. He then sat down and at the rate of fifteen handwritten letters per day thanked ever donor personally for their contributions. This habit continued throughout his life, culminating years later in hundreds of faxes back to his office from wherever he was in the world on diplomatic rugby duty.

Whilst he was not perceived generally as being a particularly hard disciplinarian, he would come down like the proverbial ton of bricks on boys being rude to kitchen staff or cleaners and 'respect for others' was an important trait he wanted to instil into all his current and future pupils. One future Test cricketer who was unsurprisingly the star of the school cricket team had the captaincy taken away from him on account of his overly critical attitude towards his less-talented teammates.

Rather like prime ministers and company CEOs, all new headmasters who wanted to change the culture of their organisation were forced to clear out some of the old guard and John's arrival at Cranbrook was no exception. On arrival he discovered that he was considerably younger than virtually the entire teaching staff but was lucky in that the majority of them bought into his new regime. Indeed, many new recruits – like James Bradnock – did so with considerable enthusiasm. Unfortunately, this was not going to be the case when the time came for John to move on to his second headmastership at the larger Eastbourne College.

However, his lasting legacy at Cranbrook was an ambitious building programme which began with that new swimming pool and then progressed to a science block, a new House for dayboys and a number of smaller projects, all of which had to be realised in the face of endless battles with the Kent education authorities over funding.

John's tenure in Kent and the advances he was advocating ensured that he was an active participant in the Headmasters' Conference – that part professional association, part political pressure group, part 'quasi-Trade Union' and part social club for the heads of independent schools in the UK. John's fame as a rugby player coupled with his youth and energy made him a likely recruitment target for many of the current public schools at the time.

In John's case Eastbourne College made a lot of sense. Not only was it larger than Cranbrook but also it was very close to Toby's old friends and, since giving birth to a fifth child, she no doubt welcomed the idea of being back in familiar surroundings.

Up until this point John's life had generally been one success followed by another, but this time he stepped into a bit of a political minefield. The chairman of the governors was very supportive of John but many of the others felt they were bringing in a 'name' who would put some extra sporting gloss onto the school and in particular its rugby team. Eastbourne College had played a significant rugby role for some years not only out on the pitch but also in acting as the pre-tour training base for major visiting touring teams such as the All Blacks and Springboks. The British Lions teams had also traditionally used the college for their own preparations before flying off overseas.

John however was keener to focus upon the academic side of things and wanted to improve several areas of underachievement. This in itself was a direct challenge to the 'status quo' and implied criticism of what the current staff had been doing – or more probably failing to do. To complicate matters further, in appointing John, the governors had rejected at least one – possibly more – internal candidate who resented being passed over. He thus found himself walking into a particularly toxic environment which he would never have suspected before he took the job.

Suffice to say that John was to spend a very unhappy couple of years which put a great strain not only upon himself and his health but also on the family. It was perhaps something of a relief when it was decided to end the relationship, and he left for what the press reported as a 'sabbatical' but probably today would be termed as 'leaving by mutual consent'.

He was not to leave unscathed. Still in his mid-forties, he suffered a heart attack and would be forced to take life relatively easily for several months.

21

Back in the Saddle

The family had recently purchased a house back in Penzance and this is where John was to spend the majority of the next year. The two elder boys were by then at boarding school – in Tim's case back at Cranbrook whilst the more sports-minded Nick went off to Clifton. The girls and Giles all went to school for a year in Penzance and as a result probably saw more of their father during that time.

As his health recovered, John was far from idle and picked up on some of his old rugby relationships with both the Cornwall Rugby Union and the English Schools organisations. He later took on the role of being secretary of the RFU's schools committee and also added to his CV by qualifying as an Associate Chartered Practitioner. Whilst looking for a new headmastership, his restless nature led him to travel the length and breadth of the country and in doing so managed to visit every cathedral in the United Kingdom. Given there are fifty-two Anglican and twenty-eight Roman Catholic ones, this was no mean feat.

In 1973 Wellington School was already a long-established independent Direct Grant school based in the middle of the small market town of the same name close to the border between Somerset and Devon. As with the case at Cranbrook, its long-term headmaster James Stredder had retired after no less than twenty-six years in the job and the governors now sought a younger, dynamic man to take the school forward in what was a difficult period for the entire country.

The Heath government was in dire trouble, the economy was in turmoil largely due to rampant inflation fuelled by a combination of appalling industrial relations and OPEC quadrupling the price of crude oil. Added to this, Northern Ireland was in flames and football matches were frequently battle zones on the terraces. Just to add to it all, the President of the United States was becoming sucked inexorably into what was soon to be known as the Watergate scandal and respect for authority was plummeting as a result. How was one to guide the minds and lives of hundreds of impressionable young teenagers in an environment such as that?

Alongside his educational career to date, John was very clearly a 'man of the world' and as such was probably much better prepared to take a lead in these circumstances than those whose lives had merely consisted of school, university and then straight back to teaching in a school again. Certainly, he had excelled whilst he was at school, but he had since served in the war, led his country on the rugby field, already travelled extensively and had naturally acquired that all-important 'presence' which anyone with pretensions towards leading a school or indeed a company is obliged to display.

Being based in the Westcountry was no doubt attractive to John as well. He was not too far from Nick at Clifton and even Penzance was comfortably reachable within three hours. Furthermore, it was halfway between Cornwall and Twickenham where his ever-increasing involvement with the RFU would soon be constantly leading him. Wellington had already just embarked upon receiving girls into the sixth form but the school clearly needed some substantial investment in its facilities. This last aspect was to be something in which he was to excel.

Taking up the role in the summer of 1973, he embarked upon a seemingly never-ending programme of rebuilding the fabric of the school and, over the next few years, managed once again to cajole huge sums of money out of alumni, local businesses and well-wishers which soon dwarfed the amounts he had managed to acquire for Cranbrook. By the time of his death in 1990 he had already completed a staggering rebuilding programme which included a dedicated House for girls, a sixth-form centre, an art room, an all-weather sports pitch, squash courts and the crowning glory of a plush modern science block which would posthumously bear his name. In all he had raised over £5 million and the school had somehow managed to do all this without incurring any debt.

He had also to gather staff around him whom he could trust and would support him as he had no wish to repeat his unhappy experiences at Eastbourne. As his time at Wellington went on, he seemed to take on yet more and more responsibilities and projects which would take him away from the school, often for quite prolonged periods of time. And yet he always needed to be kept close to whatever was going on back at the school. Because of this he required a cadre of people to whom he could not only delegate with confidence but also would not become too infuriated if he wanted to dive into the minutiae of an issue despite being thousands of miles and several time zones away.

This would not make him the easiest person to work for but as time went on, he cemented his control of the school with respect to his relationships with the Board of Governors and the school's purse strings. When the school bursar left, he almost uniquely took on the role himself, thus gaining almost complete control of all the school's affairs.

Despite gradually becoming a somewhat 'all-powerful' figure he always retained that concern for the individual, especially if they were experiencing difficulties. If he was by then in the position of an autocrat (and many headmasters in independent schools undoubtedly were), he was nevertheless an extremely benevolent one with a ready place in his heart for the 'underdog'. This powerful and attractive streak in his character would show itself when in due course he was to make the single most important rugby decision in his life.

As time moved on John took on more and more extracurricular responsibilities, not only with regard to rugby but also including the twinning of Wellington with its counterpart of the same name in the USA. That same slightly 'anorak' mentality which had taken him to visit all the cathedrals in Britain also extended to having a haircut in every town named Wellington throughout the world, the capital of New Zealand being the most obvious.

Those frequent and increasingly prolonged absences from the school meant that he depended heavily on those few trusted colleagues who could be relied upon to both deal with issues as they arose but at the same time keep him closely appraised of what was going on. This was decades before anything like 'Facetime' could be achieved on mobile phones which were still in their infancy and, even if you had one, they were the size of a house brick. Even emails and text messages – let alone internet features like WhatsApp and Twitter – were all still a couple of decades into the future. As a consequence, he would work through mountains of faxes and sought to manage as far as possible in that manner.

He was fortunate that soon after his arrival he had recruited a loyal and totally reliable secretary in Jackie Waters. It was she who was somehow able to translate his streams of faxed questions and instructions into action back on the ground and to keep him closely advised as to progress. Had this not been the case it is extremely doubtful as to whether Wellington School could have continued to operate effectively whilst John was off flying over the Pacific Ocean.

Another key appointment was that of his deputy headmaster and for this he brought in a younger man who also hailed from Penzance, named Alan Rogers. Rogers had also been to Oxford and, as a child, had watched John play rugby back in Cornwall. He had gained valuable experience both at Arnold School in Blackpool and then at Wellington College – that public school in Berkshire named in honour of the famous Duke and which is frequently mixed up in peoples' minds with Wellington School.

A deputy headship is always an extremely onerous role and, in these circumstances of frequently having to second guess his headmaster's instructions, it must have been an enormous challenge. Alan finally got his just reward when he took over the top job not long after John's untimely death in 1990.

We are however once again getting a little ahead of ourselves. As he had settled into life at Wellington back in the mid-1970s, John had felt the lure of rugby once more and this is when the pressures really began to mount.

22

The Inescapable Lure of Rugby

Whenever the time comes for a committed rugby player to finally hang up his boots for the last time it can seem almost like a bereavement and the urge for many to stay and 'put something back' into the game can be irresistible. Many take to coaching at various levels, some worthy souls become referees or club committeemen whilst a few just relapse into becoming 'Alickadoos' – those pot-bellied old bores propping up the bar and moaning about how things were 'so much better in my day. Now all they can do is blah blah blah.'

John had obviously taught rugby in his early days at Clifton which spanned his latter playing days and his final retirement from playing the sport, but by the time he had become a headmaster his energies were almost totally directed towards the academic and managerial side of his three schools. He had briefly done a stint as a BBC radio commentator (unpaid of course) but rarely watched much other rugby. His sons remarked that he seldom watched them play and never gave them much in the way of advice let alone any form of coaching. It was just not his way. It was probably his method of not putting pressure on them as the sons of famous sporting figures often have to spend their lives being told 'You're not as good as your dad.'

Once he was living away from Penzance and latterly Bath, he had no great connection with any particular club and there was no possible way he was ever going to relapse into becoming a gin-soaked old 'Alickadoo'. However, he was still well known and highly respected as an authority on rugby and, with the sport still remaining fiercely amateur, he was an obvious candidate for one or other of the various committees that ran the game. These might conceivably have been concerned with Cornwall (he later took on the presidency of the Cornwall RFU in 1984 for two years), the Laws of the game, England team selection or one or two others. The most obvious step however was as a representative of English Schools rugby and this was his first major foray into the world of rugby administration.

Schools' rugby in the UK was to suffer a setback in the late 1970s when a prolonged teachers' strike over pay resulted in many schoolmasters, who had loyally coached and accompanied their young rugby-playing pupils to matches out of hours and including weekends, were now reluctant to do so. This was particularly sad as most private schools were largely unaffected, which only served to exacerbate the impression in some quarters that rugby was in some ways a 'posh' sport.

Fortunately, hundreds of clubs up and down the country began to introduce mini-rugby for boys – and in time girls – for the first time. John was very supportive of this innovation and his friend Harvey Richards, who by now was himself a headmaster at a primary school, was instrumental in introducing this welcome new initiative to many clubs throughout Cornwall.

As mentioned, the 1970s were a particularly difficult time in the UK generally but in the limited world of adult rugby it continued much as it had always done. There were two highly successful Lions tours when they won a four-match Test series in New Zealand and repeated the trick three years later in South Africa. Wales had produced a golden generation of outstanding players who enjoyed something of a superstar profile but the sport itself carried on without any formal League structures and continued to be fiercely amateur. True there were tales about 'boot money', semi-official kit deals, etc., but the amounts involved were generally piffling and every player, even at international level, still needed to have a 'proper' job. Therefore, although rugby slowly began to encroach upon his time and energy at Wellington, it was still perfectly manageable.

The family settled down with the girls going to school in Taunton and the two elder boys progressing to university – in Nick's case to John's old Exeter College in Oxford. In the holidays both he and in due course his younger brother Giles turned out for Wellington RFC. Giles on one occasion formed a centre partnership in a Somerset Colts team with a gifted young tearaway from Bath who answered to the name of Jerry Guscott.

As the decade drew to a close, the England Schoolboys team embarked upon an exciting trip to Australia and New Zealand. As an experienced headmaster, past England player and president of the RFU Schools section, John was asked to manage the tour. Most of the players chosen were from independent private schools but a notable exception was future England scrum-half and captain Nigel Melville. According to Melville, John left all the coaching and selection side of things to the appointed coach – the highly experienced John Elders – and spent his time smoothing the path of the tour in general. However, he made one notable exception:

> Nearly all the lads already had conditional places at their chosen universities and were literally sweating on their A-level results. These were duly relayed to Mr Kendall-Carpenter who then went to great lengths to pass on to each player in turn how he had done and offered consoling advice to anyone who had not quite got the grades they had needed. When it came to me, I had to tell him that I had no plans to go to any university and whilst I hoped I had passed I really wasn't that bothered as to what grades I had got.

No doubt John would have taken all that in his stride but nevertheless the very fact that it happened demonstrated that even whilst he was on rugby duty, he could somehow never stop himself still being the headmaster and vice-versa.

The tour was judged to have been a great success not least as both Australia and New Zealand were defeated. A large proportion of the squad went on to play top club rugby with three – including Melville – later getting capped by England at senior level. John was by then almost universally highly regarded in Rugby Union circles and, having served several years on the large and unwieldy RFU committee, was elected to serve as its president for the season 1980-81.

The previous season Bill Beaumont had led an England team to a Grand Slam and had finally brought to an end several years of Welsh domination among the Home Nations. He then went on to lead the Lions in a disappointing 1-3 series defeat in South Africa. This was to prove to be the last time the Lions would go to the land of the Springboks for almost three long decades.

Among the host of items surviving in his scrapbooks at the time of his presidency was an invitation to one of those Buckingham Palace Garden parties hosted by the Queen and Prince Philip with the two daughters invited along as well.

It was also a season when the Welsh Rugby Union would be celebrating its centenary with all its attendant celebrations. Unfortunately, England were unable to repeat their success of the previous season, losing to Wales by a late penalty conceded by the future World Cup-winning manager Clive Woodward. A few weeks later they lost once again in the last minute to a hotly disputed try by France. Certainly, a modern TMO would have scrubbed it off within seconds.

In virtually all aspects of the role he succeeded and finished his time as president by returning to Argentina for a two-match series in Buenos Aires. This tour, again under captain Bill Beaumont and the management of the Grand Slam coach Mike Davis, had first been mooted back in 1973 but had been scratched due to continued political unrest, but this time was able to go ahead without undue problems. John and the team were lucky – a mere ten months later the Falklands War broke out with John's son Nick serving and fighting there as a Royal Marine temporarily attached to the Royal Engineers. On the plus side the contacts he made would have been useful in enticing Argentina back into the fold in time for the World Cup a mere five years after those hostilities had ended in the South Atlantic.

As far as running a school is concerned, being a committee man at the RFU would involve a certain number of meetings. Fortunately, living near Taunton with easy access to London by train or the M5/M4, this was not going to be too onerous and even a tour to Australasia during the school holidays was perfectly feasible.

However, the presidency of the Rugby Union was quite another matter as, in addition to all those meetings, it would also involve his attendance at an endless merry-go-round of club dinners, special matches, acting as the host to visiting dignitaries at international and other major fixtures, and so on. On top of all this he would have to give numerous media interviews and make dozens of speeches hopefully without committing any major political gaffes along the way.

The folks back in Cornwall were very proud of his appointment and that self-same old teammate Peter Michell threw a big party for him at his house outside Penzance. In doing so Michell had managed to gather together lots of ex-colleagues dating back to John's earliest days of playing rugby. That same weekend John had assembled another of those 'President's XV's' with a smattering of current rugby stars to take on the Pirates. Bath then held a similar dinner honouring both himself and Alec Lewis to which virtually the entire team of their era made an appearance.

The Cornish have their own special way of honouring their distinguished members by making them Bards of the Gorsedd. Essentially the Gorsedd aims to promote not only the continued survival of the Cornish language but also its poetry, music and literature and as such has a rough approximation to the Welsh Eisteddfod and a similar Celtic organisation in Brittany. That summer they conferred the honour upon John. Newly appointed Bards are dressed in traditional robes and are then given a special bardic name. John's chosen Cornish name was *'Onen a Bymthek'* which reflected both his rugby achievements and a certain modesty in that it can be translated into English as 'One of the Fifteen'.

After an exhausting stint as RFU president, most men would have contented themselves with being a venerated Immediate Past President, having the best seats and eating sumptuous dinners at international matches and being feted as something of an *eminence grise* around Twickenham. Furthermore, there was much to do at Wellington. Not so John. He was soon invited to be one of the RFU's representatives on the IRFB – then the overarching body in control of rugby across the world. If a World Cup was ever to emerge this would be the vehicle which would make it happen. Clearly there was a lot more still to come.

23

Global Rugby and Two Rogue Elephants

By the time that John moved across to join the IRFB there were already two very large elephants sitting menacingly in the rugby room. The first was the continual horror among the powers that be about the perceived creeping erosion of amateurism. Second was how the sport should deal with South Africa which was by then being noisily condemned and boycotted across virtually the entire world for its apartheid policies.

By the last quarter of the twentieth century the sport of rugby union was widely spread across what had once been the British Empire and had flourished particularly where a temperate climate was reasonably conducive to playing the game. This included South Africa, Australia and of course New Zealand where it had long been a national obsession. Additionally, many people in France – smarting from its humiliation in the Franco-Prussian War – had turned in the late nineteenth century to rugby with its ethos of teamwork, manly courage and controlled violence as an antidote to the slightly effete world of late nineteenth-century Paris. This was particularly true in the south and probably continues to this day.

With all this in mind the four 'Home Unions' comprising England, Wales, Scotland and Ireland were joined by South Africa, New Zealand and Australia in what became known as the International Rugby Football Board. It was only some years after the Second World War that the French were belatedly invited to join the Anglo-Saxons. Each nation could nominate two members to represent its own Union in all the deliberations and decisions.

As with FIFA in football, much of its best work was to ensure a common set of rules (or Laws as rugby prefers to call them) but for its entire existence it had agreed upon one core principle as though handed down to Moses on a tablet of stone: 'THOU SHALT REMAIN STRICTLY AMATEUR ALL THE DAYS OF THY LIFE'.

Of course, it wasn't phrased quite like that but for all intents and purposes it might just as well have been. Anyone who took the dreaded shekel, even in the most minor way, would be condemned, if not to a fiery furnace, then to a lifetime ban from playing or coaching Rugby Union for the rest of his life. Even entering a rugby club or running around with some children on a rugby pitch was then rendered out of bounds. What about my human rights? Forget it!

But by now we were into the last quarter of the twentieth century. Cricket, tennis, equestrianism, sailing and just about all the other slightly middle-class sports had by then allowed its best players to earn a living from their skills but rugby men somehow saw the world entirely differently. We have already seen how John's mind could bridge both a continuing commitment to amateurism (which he espoused until the day he died) and an acceptance of a man's right to go off and play Rugby League if he so wanted. What he loathed was all the hypocrisy.

So, it came about that just after he had completed his stint as RFU president, he was asked to become one of England's representatives on that sixteen-man International Board. Despite all the myriad calls upon his time he accepted and joined a former England teammate named Albert Agar to take up the cudgels on England's behalf.

By this time the sport of Rugby Union had spread far beyond those eight countries. Leading the 'wannabees' were Japan, Italy, Romania and Argentina but there were many others including Canada, USA and the Soviet Union (as it then still was) who all had growing numbers of clubs, colleges and military establishments enthusiastically taking up the sport. The USSR then still included Georgia, where the wrestling-loving locals enjoyed nothing better than a good scrum.

Then there were the Pacific Islanders embracing Fiji, Samoa, Tonga and the Cook Islands. They all bred seriously big men whose physiques were not well suited to soccer but were perfect for the game of rugby. Whatever they lacked in money and facilities they more than made up for with boundless enthusiasm and a thrilling willingness to attack from all over the field. This made them a popular draw at the turnstiles and especially when shown on television.

If you began to spread the net a bit wider still, then Zimbabwe, Kenya, Namibia, Morocco, Spain, Holland, Uruguay, Nigeria, Sri Lanka, Hong Kong and Portugal all had plenty of keen but often sadly impoverished rugby clubs.

As we have seen, John was already a widely travelled man who had developed a keen sense of helping the underdog. He saw clearly the many benefits if the ethos, camaraderie and physical endeavour of rugby could, and indeed should, be spread across the globe. Perhaps there was even a touch of the missionary in all this. He could certainly envision how Rugby Union might become a truly international sport – although perhaps not quite as much as soccer which had the double benefits of being less physically aggressive and far easier for the casual participant or spectator to understand. Whether he would have welcomed the explosion of women's rugby is of course purely hypothetical but no doubt he would have given it serious consideration and probably his keen support had he been spared another twenty years of life.

There can have been no doubt that any widely televised world competition would be a great shop window for the sport to many thousands – and probably millions – of young men and boys who might potentially take up the game. The issue was whether those charged with running the game were more interested in wanting the sport to grow or essentially to keep things more or less as they were. The various International Unions had all played against the likes of Argentina, Romania and Japan from time to time but had rather sniffily not awarded those much-prized 'caps' to the players taking part. This was on the basis that they were somehow not 'proper' international matches, which rather illustrates the then current line of thought.

One additional worry among potential naysayers for anything like a World Cup was that if rugby players absented themselves from their jobs in order to take part, then demand for some sort of broken time payments would become necessary. This of course was the very issue which had spawned the breakaway Rugby League a century before. The fallacy of this argument was that for decades the British Lions, Springboks and All Blacks had all sent their unpaid players away for lengthy four-month tours whereas any putative World Cup would all be done and dusted within about six weeks.

What about South Africa? As we know John had toured the country back in 1951 and, whilst the world had moved on over the intervening thirty years, South Africa appeared to have been stuck in something of a cultural time warp. Over that time the apartheid laws had become ever more restricting and world opinion, which had been first horrified by the Sharpeville massacre in 1960, had since become increasingly hostile, which in turn led to demonstrations, trade and sporting boycotts and the country being expelled from the Commonwealth.

On the other hand, if South Africa was not the actual number one rugby country in the entire world, then it was very close to being so. For several years the rugby authorities had tried to duck the issue behind bland statements like 'we should not let politics interfere with sport' or 'it is far better to keep contacts going than to ignore them'. Whilst both statements may have some merit in themselves, matters had by then moved on. Despite widely reported demonstrations back in Britain, the Lions had travelled to South Africa as late as 1980. Conversely the government in New Zealand had by then moved on from meekly omitting Māori and South Sea Island players from touring there to now becoming one of its shrillest critics.

By the time a potential World Cup was up for consideration it was generally recognised – even by the likes of leading rugby powerhouses Danie Craven and Louis Luyt in the Republic itself – that South Africa could never realistically be allowed to participate. From a narrow rugby perspective this was a great shame as no eventual winner could legitimately claim to be 'World Champions' if the men in the green jerseys hadn't even been there. Some naysayers even claimed that could be a reason in itself not to press ahead.

There were of course plenty of other concerns on rugby legislators' minds. Football had introduced its first World Cup way back in 1930 but it had hardly been a global phenomenon at the time. It had been tucked away down in little Uruguay during the middle of a global trade recession and an era when teams would still have to travel there for weeks by sea and so the competition was predictably dominated by the South Americans. All the United Kingdom nations shunned the competition entirely and sadly the first three World Cups took place without a single British player ever being involved.

Added to this, several of football's World Cups had suffered from quite a few dirty matches especially when headstrong Latin temperaments were involved exacerbated by political jingoism and matches occurring within very short time spans. Rugby Union in the late 1970s and early 1980s was itself going through a particularly violent period with many televised international matches degenerating into barely controlled running brawls. If mayhem was to keep breaking out on TV screens this would surely do the sport far more harm than good.

In view of this would the rugby public take to the idea? Would the television companies be interested? What would the players themselves feel about it? Would overseas fans travel thousands of miles to support their teams? With the benefit of hindsight, we now know all the answers to these questions but it was anything but clear at the time.

There was probably one other factor gnawing away in the minds of the mandarins at Twickenham, Dublin, Cardiff and particularly Edinburgh. Each Union held virtually unchallenged power to control the sport in so far as it affected their own countrymen. A putative World Cup would necessarily involve them ceding a fair bit of that control to an external global body.

That would have made them even more uneasy.

24

A World Cup –
Stick or Twist?

The idea of some sort of worldwide rugby competition was nothing new. In the first quarter of the twentieth century it had even been included in the Olympic Games. Indeed, Cornwall as the current county champions had represented Britain in 1908 in a fogbound match at the White City. This was until its founder, the all-powerful Baron de Coubertin (who was rumoured to have been a big rugby fan), had very reluctantly decided to scratch it from future Games. This came after a Final between France and the victorious USA at Paris in 1924 had culminated in a mass brawl involving spectators as well as players. Even today Olympic rugby is limited to seven-a-side competitions.

At the latter stages of both World Wars there had been some very unofficial international tournaments in Europe involving servicemen from the various allied forces which included Australians, New Zealanders (the famous Kiwis), South African and Canadian forces as well as their British and French counterparts. In 1917 there had even been a 'Somme Cup' which, as might be expected, landed up somewhere in New Zealand. However, everybody soon went back home and that was the end of it.

As early as the 1960s a tentative suggestion for some sort of international tournament had been made by two Australians named Jock Kellaher and Harold Tolhurst. They had floated the idea but it had predictably been ignored. However, by 1980 just about every major team sport had a world championship of some sort. Rugby League had introduced one back in 1954, hockey in 1971 and finally cricket, with many of the same nations involved, got underway in 1975.

Rugby Union once more had stood out as an exception. Club rugby in the UK had still not adopted a system of Leagues, so every match was nominally a 'friendly'. France had administered its own competition for many years and there was the Currie Cup in South Africa and the Ranfurly Shield in New Zealand. However, all that 'cups and medals' stuff wasn't to the taste of those gentlemen who ran the various Home Unions.

Then things began to change rapidly largely driven from Australia with New Zealand very soon becoming an enthusiastic ally. The game in Oz was losing its best players seemingly every month to the locally far more popular – and professional – Rugby League. In fact, the Union game was something of a poor relation in that it lagged in popular appeal behind cricket, rugby league, 'Aussie rules', horse racing and even surfing. It desperately needed something special in order to widen its appeal to a sports-crazy public.

Next South Africa, by now considered beyond the pale as far as international rugby was concerned and thus feeling the pinch, had whispered quietly but menacingly about introducing professionalism as an antidote to falling interest. They had recently undertaken a miserable tour to New Zealand where they had been pelted with flour bombs, buzzed by light aircraft, abused and spat at by anti-apartheid demonstrators who had the added comfort of knowing that the New Zealand government was basically on their side. Nevertheless, to Dr Craven and his acolytes some sort of global competition would have sounded extremely attractive if only they could be allowed to take part.

A decade earlier an Australian TV mogul named Kerry Packer, aided by England's South African-born captain Tony Greig, had thrown the world of cricket into turmoil by signing up dozens of leading Test Match players to participate in a series of commercialised matches, rather sarcastically referred to by the media as a 'circus'. The bigwigs of cricket went into a brief meltdown, introduced some major changes, most of the players returned to the fold and the problem soon went away.

Now another Australian media man by the name of David Lord had come up with a plan to sign up a couple of hundred international rugby players to participate in a travelling international competition. Once again this sent shudders down the spines of rugby administrators around the globe. As a result, the prospect of any World Cup was going to get horribly tangled up with all the age-old paranoia about creeping professionalism.

At this point it is probably worth referring to the minutes of the IRFB at the time. At a meeting on 11 March 1983 one of the items on the agenda was to consider a proposal from a company called Lloyd International fronted by a well-known former cricketer and sports commentator named Neil Durden-Smith.

Tucked away inside reams of discussion about amateurism, book writing (some leading players including the recently retired England hero Bill Beaumont had gone to print and understandably wanted their share of the royalties), kit design and dining protocols (yes really!) there is the following small item:

World Cup Competition
In the light of approaches to all Member Unions by a company of sports promoters the question was considered as to whether the Board supported a World Cup Competition. The concept found no support.

Despite the sniffy tone of that terse minute, those around the table were shrewd enough to know that the days of merely playing King Canute were fast coming to an end and that the issue was not going to go away. Furthermore, there was a steely determination that if any World Cup was ever to come to fruition it should be run by true rugby people and not some entrepreneurs on the lookout for making a fast buck. The determination on this particular point was equally shared by the men in the Southern Hemisphere. Nobody wanted to see any sort of rugby version of the Harlem Globetrotters.

As a result, a small Home Unions Emergency Committee was set up – which now included John – to look into the matter a little deeper. Tellingly this group brought together John and Keith Rowlands, a slightly younger ex-Wales and Lions lock forward who by then worked as the commercial director for Taunton Cider. Their combined sense of friendship and shared vision would soon prove to be crucial.

The outcome was nevertheless entirely negative and in July an equally terse press statement was issued to the effect that,

> The Board reiterated the view that an 'International Tournament' had no support and that rugby would survive the challenge of any potential circus.

At the time, England's pair of nominees to the IRFB had been two distinguished ex-England players who were both contemporaries of John. They were that former Harlequins centre Albert Agar and the very well-known Barbarian committee man Mickey Steele-Bodger. The following year Steele-Bodger (who had for a while been IRFB chairman) stepped down on a rotational basis to be replaced by John. He would now be one of the key decision makers on any major aspects of world rugby – including any potential plans for a World Cup.

At this point it is probably appropriate to review the membership of that powerful group. It is also worth stating that they were 'nominees' of the constituent countries rather than mere 'delegates'. In other words, whilst they would naturally be expected to reflect the views of the nation they represented, they were more or less entitled to vote as they saw fit. In fact, it was all a bit secretive and official records as to who voted for what generally remained under wraps.

The Board at that time was comprised as follows:

The chairman, Dr Vanderveld with Turnbull (both Australia), Ferrasse and Bosc (France), Blazey and Stuart (New Zealand), Albert Agar and now John (England), McKibbin and Dawson (Ireland), Dr.Craven and Eloff (South Africa), Rowlands and Treharne (Wales), Burrell and Connor (Scotland).

A joint Feasibility Study had already been undertaken by the New Zealanders and Australians and they had circulated their findings in advance to all the members of the Board. This essentially recommended that an initial competition be hosted jointly by New Zealand and Australia in June/July of 1987. Some sixteen nations would be invited which was to include all the IRB countries (with the obvious exception of South Africa) plus Italy, Japan, Argentina, Canada, United States, Fiji, Tonga, Romania and Zimbabwe.

John would have already known one or two of them slightly. Bob Stuart was an old friend from his time leading the 1953 All Blacks to Britain, Ronnie Dawson had led the Lions to New Zealand in 1959 and he would have played against George Burrell when he had appeared as the Scotland full-back.

The key meeting was to be held in March at the HQ of the French railways in Paris hosted by their veteran wheeler-dealer Albert Ferrasse. France had only been received into the IRFB as recently as 1978 having previously been the leading light in the organisation that covered all the 'other countries' named the FIRA. Ferrasse would therefore potentially carry a great deal of influence upon countries such as Italy, Romania and Argentina and it was common knowledge that the French were already broadly in favour of the competition going ahead.

His French colleague on the Board was Andre Bosc who was a senior executive with the self-same railway, which probably explains the venue. On the day of the crucial vote Bosc treated all the Board members to a luxury trip on France's swanky new TGV down to the gastronomic paradise that is Lyon for a slap-up lunch, no doubt accompanied by bucketloads of vintage French wine. On returning to Paris in the late afternoon for the vital meeting he had at least ensured that everyone was in a mellow mood. The party included Dr Danie Craven who was going to make damned sure that South Africa would have its say in any decision on the matter, even if they would be debarred from competing themselves for the time being.

Any decision to proceed with a World Cup would require a clear majority in favour and, with the eight Board Member countries each having two votes, the indicators were that was going to be virtually impossible to achieve. Ferrasse and Craven had thrown their support in with the Australians and New Zealanders but the Home Unions i.e., England, Wales, Ireland and Scotland had all declared against the proposal going ahead. In other words, with eight 'ayes' and in all likelihood eight 'nays', the voting would result in a stalemate and any credible World Cup would be stillborn. The consequences were potentially horrible for rugby as a deep thinker such as John would have been all too aware.

What would have happened if the proposal had been stymied by a cartel of recalcitrant Brits? Rugby had suffered one catastrophic schism leading to Rugby League a hundred years before and still bore the scars. The 'Yes vote' faction might conceivably have tried to launch a diminished competition on their own and via FIRA would in all probability have attracted the support of the Italians, Argentinians, Fijians, etc. in doing so. Like football in 1930, Britain would then be left sitting impotently on the sidelines and the IRFB itself would have become irrelevant.

What if on the rebound the Southern Hemisphere had then allowed some form of limited professionalism in spite of the North? There would almost certainly have been a second drain of talent 'going south' to places like Sydney in addition to the existing drip-feed of players 'going north' to the likes of Wigan and St Helens. If an appreciable number of the best UK players had done so the appeal of the then Five Nations would obviously be compromised massively.

Furthermore, if relationships had then been allowed to become sufficiently acrimonious what future – if any – would there be for the British and Irish Lions? Would the two factions soon develop different interpretations of the Laws of the game, something the IRFB had worked slavishly to improve for many years?

All these things – and probably quite a few more – would have raced through John's fertile brain and then there was something else. On a more positive note, he was one of the precious few at a senior level in the game who had a vision of how rugby could become a truly global sport. Along with this he would also have instinctively realised that, if only its core values of hard physical combat combined with decency, respect and participation for enjoyment, lifelong friendship and playing for fun rather than financial reward could somehow be preserved, it could be a real force for good in an increasingly cynical and mercenary sporting world.

Remember also John's constant championing of the underdog which had guided him all through his adult life. He had been to countries like Italy and Argentina and understood fully how the game in these places was desperately short not only of money but also close involvement at all levels not least in the area of coaching. What about where the game was actually struggling just to survive in places like Georgia, Malaysia and Tonga? Sitting there obsessed with preserving a highly dubious and inwardly looking status quo would have been counter to every value he had cherished since he was a little boy back in Cornwall.

He took a deep breath and voted 'Yes'.

25

Politics and Making
It Happen

As it turned out John was not entirely isolated as his friend Keith Rowlands also switched one if not both of the Welsh votes, so the result is believed to have been 10-6 or even 12-4 in favour. The term 'believed' is necessary as the precise votes had remained confidential but the essential outcome was effectively one with six countries declaring in favour with only two (Ireland and Scotland) opposed.

John of course knew he would face a barrage of criticism from inside the RFU back at Twickenham but neither he nor Rowlands were sacked. Indeed, most of the rugby press were both surprised and delighted that somebody in authority had possessed the *cojones* to look forwards rather than continually driving in their rear mirror. Naturally he got a few 'Judas' type remarks from some of the naysayers. Conversely, there were a significant number of committeemen who would have quietly applauded what he had done but had not been prepared to put their own heads above the parapet.

The Scots, who were traditionally the most ultra-conservative Union on the planet, were the most unhappy. One prominent Scotsman who shall remain nameless had blithely informed John before the vote that, 'A World Cup will come in over my dead body!'

When they happened to bump into one another a few weeks later John's cheery greeting was, 'Hello are you still alive?'

Meanwhile the Irish, generally in agreement with the position of the Scots, took a while to accept the *fait accompli* but gradually did so and fell into line.

So, what was John's reward? A World Cup Steering Committee was set up and John was voted to chair it. He must soon have wondered what the hell he had let himself in for. He was joined on this Steering Committee by Keith Rowlands, Ronnie Dawson, Bob Stuart and Ross Turnbull and they immediately got down to work.

The organisers had no money, no offices, no professional staff and no corporate structure, so virtually everything had to be built from scratch. John quietly approached Dudley Wood, the secretary of the RFU to become the IRFB World Cup secretary, but Wood had only been in his current job for less than two years and he had more than enough on his plate with the total rebuilding of Twickenham and so he politely declined.

The Steering Committee clearly needed some big men on the ground down in the Antipodes to kickstart the whole process and by this time there was only a painfully short twenty-three-month window before the first ball was to be kicked off. Of course, a whole host of characters soon became involved but three in particular need to be identified.

The first is Sir Nicholas Shehadie, a larger-than-life ex-prop forward who had toured the UK with Australia back in 1947 and again in 1957 and who had been honoured to be picked for the Barbarians to play against those self-same Wallabies. Since retiring from rugby he had built up a very successful motor-related business and had served as the Lord Mayor of Sydney.

The second was Dick Littlejohn, a Kiwi from the Bay of Plenty region who had previously managed the All Blacks and had fulfilled just about every position imaginable on the New Zealand rugby scene. He certainly knew his way around the country, all the pressmen, business leaders, potential sponsors and local mayors, etc. and would thus prove vital in getting things off the ground in the ridiculously short time available.

Those two had already toured around Britain during that year's Five Nations Championship in what was dubbed in the newspapers as the 'Dick and Nick Show'. They were promoting that feasibility study with which they had been trying desperately to get the rugby powers that be in Britain to support the World Cup concept. More often than not they had been received politely but constantly ran into a depressingly large percentage of closed minds.

The third key figure was Cecil Blazey, who had spent a lifetime in the administration of rugby in New Zealand with his service in various capacities stretching back to the late 1930s and who had been a member of the New Zealand Rugby Executive since 1957. He was widely recognised as the wise old owl of Kiwi rugby and his involvement and support for the new venture would also prove to be invaluable.

Those three in particular – plus of course a fourth in Bob Stuart – became really close friends with John, who frequently visited their homes and families where they shared many a beer and laugh together. Those tight bonds of mutual respect among the four of them would become super-important when all the organisational stresses and strains accompanied by all the carping from an unsympathetic media began to bite.

Before long that steering committee had been slimmed down to three members with John in the chair being joined by Shehadie and Littlejohn and registered as a formal Company named 'Rugby World Cup Pty'. This achieved three things. Firstly, it gave real power to the local men down in Australia and New Zealand and secondly the ability to enter into formal contracts with sponsors, marketing organisations, travel and ticketing agencies, etc. Finally, the term 'Pty' is short for 'proprietary' and limits legal liability in Australia, roughly like 'Ltd' does in the UK.

Those immediate issues for this new company were having no money of its own, no paid employees and, with John in particular, needing to travel very long distances. These were addressed rapidly with a couple of essentially exhibition games being staged that April at Twickenham and Cardiff. The British Lions (not yet to be dubbed by the more politically correct but cumbersome name of 'British and Irish Lions') were planned to tour South Africa in 1986. This was of course by then a dead duck but an unofficial quasi-Lions squad was assembled which twice took on an equally unofficial 'Rest of World' team, one which perversely included a smattering of Springboks. Everyone seemed happy and 'Rugby World Cup Pty' now had about half a million pounds in its coffers.

Now it was all systems go – or at least it was 'Down Under'. Movement in the UK often proceeded with the glacial speed adopted by the Civil Service and Sir Humphrey Appleby of the hit TV programme *Yes Minister* which was enormously popular at the time. Frankly many old boys in senior rugby positions still seemed to hope that if they kept their heads down long enough it would somehow all just go away.

The RFU minutes from early 1986 shed further light on all this continual carping when it states baldly that,

> Concern was voiced about the lack of information on the commercial aspects of the World Cup and who would have to underwrite any financial loss on the venture.

John's terse reply was that he was perfectly happy to let them know who the sponsors would be and that, by the way, they certainly expected the World Cup to make a profit.

This dragged on all the way through 1986 – only a matter of months before the World Cup was due to start. As late as that autumn some RFU members were *still* trying to hold back the tide and insist that they hadn't yet formally agreed that England would actually send out a team to compete.

This sense of denial was illustrated graphically in the RFU minutes of October 1986.

> As far as the RFU were concerned it was AGREED (note capitals) that there was a need for the full committee to confirm or otherwise their (i.e., England's) participation in the 1987 World Cup and thereafter to be signed accordingly.

On yet another occasion the RFU minutes expressed

> their grave concern that the Keith Prowse Organisation had already been awarded the ticketing agency and that no separate allocation had been made for those taking part.

It was by then quite clear that the Home Unions could see that any control they may have still imagined they had over events was slipping inexorably away by the week. They had nevertheless re-confirmed John's position as an England representative on the IRFB but had now also appointed as his England colleague Brigadier Dennis Shuttleworth, who was felt to be one of the many RFU sceptics on the matter of the World Cup in general.

The following month John was away in Japan negotiating a major sponsorship deal and his place at the RFU committee meeting was taken by the ex-England centre Mike Weston who was then the current England chief coach. He would thus be leading any England team in the competition. He did his best to reassure the waverers and naysayers with a lot of graphs and pictures of all the preparations now fully underway in New Zealand and Australia.

The committee were however predictably upset on being informed at their December meeting that the Rugby World Cup Pty had already signed a whole raft of legally binding contracts before the RFU had been able to take a vote on it. They felt they were being railroaded, which of course was by then undeniably true.

All this was still going around in circles as the final decision on whether England would compete or not was only finally decided in January 1987 – less than five months before the competition was due to start. That decision was at long last to participate although it was still left up for debate as to whether any match in the World Cup would qualify for a 'cap' or not.

When the England team did finally manage to take off for Australia support still appeared to have been given extremely grudgingly. Weston was only allowed to take twenty-six players plus a coach, doctor, fitness adviser and one physiotherapist and moreover he was not paid for his pains.

Similar tortuous committee meetings would have taken place in Wales, Ireland and particularly Scotland but somehow by the end of the season all four nations were preparing to fly south and take part.

This deep divide between the gung-ho brigade down in Australia and New Zealand, straining every sinew to get things going, and a lot of decidedly negative characters back in Britain was to cause John a great deal of stress and heartache. He would soon be suffering from both this incessant sniping back in Britain and a lot of extremely aggressive criticism in the Australian and particularly New Zealand media. As our cricketers and touring British Lions have often discovered, there is nothing that these folk seem to enjoy more than a bit of 'pommy-bashing' and a tall, upright Englishman with a fancy double-barrelled surname was easy prey.

Just what he was up against can be gleaned from a New Zealand rugby annual from 1987 which baldly stated,

> Australia, supported by New Zealand had first mooted the idea of a World Rugby Tournament early in the 1980's but it took some time and a great deal of persuasion to get the conservative Home-Unions-influenced IRB to accept the concept.

So far so good – but then it got personal.

> If the IRB did reluctantly agree that such a radical rugby festival take place it did its best to sabotage the event by insisting that the organising committee was chaired by England's John Kendall-Carpenter.
>
> A pedantic committee man , Kendall-Carpenter did little to endear himself to the Australasian media on his trips to the Antipodes and found himself on the receiving end of many outraged articles including the fiasco of ticket prices.

This sort of bile – and it was sometimes a lot worse – was not only grossly unfair but also was frequently just plain nasty.

26

When the Going Gets Tough

At the time that all this was going on, a major Hollywood blockbuster called *The Jewel of the Nile* had come out with a catchy theme song by Billy Ocean which became a massive hit all around the world. It was of course 'When the Going Gets Tough, the Tough Get Going' and this seemed tailor-made for the position in which John was now to find himself.

Underlying and exacerbating all of this was the fact that John was still in an extremely demanding full-time job as a headmaster back in Wellington. At the risk of repetition, it has to be understood that this was at a time when the internet, e-mails, mobile phones, simple dial-up conference calls, Skype and Zoom were yet to appear. Whole rafts of people nevertheless had to be consulted, countries scattered across the globe had to be visited, political issues smoothed over and meetings chaired. On top of this the tournament was being held far away on the exact far side the globe involving thirty-hour flights or even more if the journey was to be broken by a stop along the way. There is a saying that 'if you want a job done you should give it to a busy man', but surely this was pushing it.

At this stage it is probably worth considering how well suited he was to the role he had been given at such short notice. The issues facing the competition could perhaps be broken down into three major components. There would be firstly political, secondly business/financial, and thirdly logistical aspects of getting such a thing as a World Cup off the ground.

Provided that he could somehow continue to keep the school on track and his governors acquiescent, then he was probably well suited for the first. He was widely travelled, open to new ideas, looked the part, chose his words carefully and had a keen sense of empathy with those from a different background than himself.

A good example of this is Japan which, of all the modern first world post-industrial nations, is probably from a cultural point of view the least like the UK. The leading light of Japanese rugby at the time was a gentleman by the name of 'Shiggy' Konno. He was exactly the same age as John, had been sent as a child to a preparatory school in Surrey and hence spoke fluent English and was extremely enthusiastic about the prospect of Japan being at last able to compete at rugby on a world stage. They had one other thing in common as they had both trained as pilots in the latter stage of the war but had not actually been called upon to go into action. In Shiggy's case this was probably just as well as he would laughingly describe himself as a 'Kamikaze pilot – failed'.

John travelled unceasingly around the globe meeting up with rugby men from Tokyo to Tbilisi and Bucharest to Buenos Aires and somehow getting them onside with what was expected. He of course had to liaise closely with the men on the ground like Littlejohn, Shehadie, Stuart and the rest. Occasionally they could meet up somewhere roughly halfway like Hong Kong or Kuala Lumpur but to say it was an exhausting business was to put it mildly. All the time he would be carrying briefcases bulging with school reports, letters, accounts, etc. For years he had been accustomed to working way into the small hours but how he was able to get through all of this work despite the inevitable jet lag frankly beggars belief.

On the second area he was obviously well outside of his comfort zone. He had of course been acting as his school's bursar but he was essentially a historian rather than an accountant. On the commercial side he had undertaken protracted negotiations with educational authorities in Kent and Somerset raising the money for several building projects but had absolutely no first-hand business experience of matters such as marketing, advertising, ticketing, media relations, etc. In fact, most of this was to be outsourced to consultancies and overseen by the men on the ground in New Zealand. Similarly, with all the thousands of logistical details to be resolved, he would clearly need to rely on the specialists on the spot. Nevertheless, as the man in the top seat he would need to fully understand and appreciate whatever was taking place and be able to defend it as necessary.

The company appointed to find and negotiate for sponsors, television rights, travel concessions, etc. was West Nally, who had probably secured the contract against other suitors by allegedly guaranteeing $5 million to the organisers. This it will be recalled was the organisation chaired by Peter West, one of his old governors from his days back in Cranbrook. The main 'mover and shaker' in that organisation was a thrusting young Englishman named Patrick Nally who was building a big reputation in bringing international business and sport together hopefully for mutual financial benefit.

Thirty-five years later almost every shirt, hoarding and even pitches have a sponsor's logo splattered across them whilst stadiums and trophies adopt product names seemingly without batting an eyelid. Back in the 1980s this was all very new and, as with most of these initiatives, would have been viewed with considerable unease, even in the Southern Hemisphere.

By 1985 Nally, still then in his late thirties, had already developed an enviable portfolio of clients as varied as the FIFA World Cup, the London Marathon and tours by the Rolling Stones. He would surely have occupied another universe than those old RFU boys back in the East India Club, so it was natural that his links would have to have been forged between his colleague on the spot – Michael Storey – and the businessmen based in Sydney and Auckland.

With Japan's booming economy, burgeoning love of rugby and its enthusiasm for a World Cup it was perhaps unsurprising that the major sponsor would turn out to be a Japanese telecommunications company called Kokusai Denshin Denwa (KDD) and it is conceivable that John's association with Shiggy Konno might have helped. This was fortunate as West Nally had been struggling.

Others followed in its wake including Rank Xerox, Mazda and the Auckland brewery Steinlager. Another problem cropped up in that all the sponsors insisted upon what were termed 'clean stadiums', which meant there could be no other advertising sited in the stadium or in the sightline of television cameras. This caused a big furore in Australia to the extent that the Sydney Cricket Ground, which was still where the majority of Rugby Union tests were held, declared itself out of bounds and the organisers were forced to settle for the more downbeat Concord Oval.

In fact, rugby in the UK had already been dipping its toes gingerly into sponsorship for some time. It had quietly 'forfeited its virginity' fifteen years earlier with the then new RFU knock-out cup being named after cigarette manufacturers John Player and by 1987 the new Leagues in England and Scotland were associated with brewers John Courage and McEwan's respectively. The Hong Kong Sevens were financially tied up with the Cathay Pacific airline, the County Championship with Thorn TV, and so it went on.

Just to add to the range of difficulties John faced were two further unrelated issues, one political the other medical. In the middle of all the negotiations a team of All Blacks in all but name and shirt colour defied both the NZRFU and their government by undertaking an unofficial tour of South Africa. They were called the Cavaliers and were managed by two of New Zealand's true rugby legends, Colin Meads and Ian Kirkpatrick. Only two prominent current players turned it down – David Kirk (the man destined to lift the trophy a year later) and star winger John Kirwan. This meant that if all those players who did go to South Africa were banned for defying the authorities, then the All Blacks would be going into the competition with a virtual Second XV which would have made the whole thing a farce.

What made it worse was that those tourists would undoubtedly have received substantial compensation – possibly cloaked in the form of extremely generous 'expenses' – for going. Just to add to this another prominent current All Black had recently appeared in a television advert in New Zealand and had been paid for his trouble. If only two or three of the current big-name players had been involved, they would in all probability have been cast aside, but there was safety in numbers and the New Zealand public not only wanted the competition to take place, but they also badly wanted to win it. If they were to be shorn of the services of the likes of Wayne Shelford, Murray Mexted and Grant Fox they were likely to struggle.

Whilst this was a domestic crisis in New Zealand, the fact that all they got was a rap on the knuckles and allowed to remain in the fold was a clear setback for global unity. Three of the invitees to the World Cup were to be Zimbabwe plus Fiji and Tonga who, as part of the Commonwealth, had all recently opposed Margaret Thatcher's position of retaining at least some trade with South Africa. They were now rumoured to be unhappy about playing in a tournament involving players who had defied their own government and gone to play there. This was smoothed over in due course and all duly took part but was yet another major headache for the poor chairman of the World Cup.

In fact, everywhere he looked John would have been acutely aware of political sensitivities which might blight the competition at the outset. The British and the Argentinians had been at war with one another over the Falklands a mere five years before. Romania was still under the brutal regime of Nicolae Ceausescu and several of their players would have been either part of the army or his Securitate secret police. Meanwhile Robert Mugabe's then new policy of commandeering white-owned farms in Zimbabwe was starting to make lurid headlines following its recent brutal civil war.

It was also believed that the Rugby World Cup – presumably via John – had approached the Soviet Union which at that time not only included rugby-loving Georgia but also had a small but growing cadre of rugby clubs in Russia itself. Nothing came of this, probably due to the fact that Moscow was still reeling from its ill-fated military venture into Afghanistan, had only recently appointed Mikhail Gorbachev as its new leader and in 1986 had just suffered the appalling tragedy at Chernobyl. They probably had more on their minds than making up the numbers in a faraway rugby tournament.

Another non-political – but still global – issue had also cropped up and that was the appearance of the AIDS virus. It was thought to have been around in parts of Africa for a little while but shot to world attention when American film actor Rock Hudson had died from it in late 1985. At that point no cure had as yet been developed and, whilst it never shut down half the world as Covid-19 was to do a generation later, both the media and the population in general were very frightened as to where it might lead. In fact, it never had any impact on the Rugby World Cup but must have posed an additional headache at the time.

As with any new venture, money was going to be a potential source of squabbling but a deal was finally struck in March 1986 which gave the two hosts 100 percent of the gate money and 48 percent of the commercial and television income. The other participants would divide the rest between them. This seemed to be considered generally fair as the two host countries were bearing the brunt of the administrative costs. Furthermore, the Australians insisted that West Nally paid their $5 million up front, which turned out to be fortuitous as the company went down in a stock market crash a mere three months after the tournament ended.

Already mentioned was the nagging concern that a heady mix of high emotions and varying temperaments would lead to some overly rough play which might tarnish the reputation of the entire sport. This was especially concerning if it was to be screened to millions of men, women and particularly children around the world who had probably never seen a game of rugby before. Rugby in the early 1980s was going through an especially brutal phase and, whilst the British were always keen to lay any blame for this onto the laps of everyone else, they needed to look carefully into the mirror themselves. Just a couple of months before the tournament kicked off a Wales v England match had been punctuated by a series of unsavoury brawls in front of another huge

TV audience. Fortunately, despite a sending off or two these fears also turned out to be largely unfounded.

There was one other little issue to confront the upcoming World Cup – there wasn't one! Accordingly, John duly turned up one afternoon at Garrards the jewellers – then in London's Regent Street – and picked out a fine piece of Victorian gilded silver which was to be known as the 'Webb Ellis Cup' with all its historical connotations. Weighing 108 ounces, it had all the look and feel of a substantial trophy and for once met with unanimous approval from all concerned. It apparently cost around £5,000, which seems a pretty good bargain for all the excitement and pleasure it has generated over the past four decades.

Today such a highly prized trophy would be transported across the globe with maximum security, special documentation and due pomp and ceremony. According to John's daughter Diana, who has lived in New Zealand for many years, her father simply stuffed the Webb Ellis Cup into one of his bulging suitcases held in place by a dozen pairs of, presumably clean, socks.

As he criss-crossed the globe spinning all these plates, he was still running a growing school back in Wellington. A seasoned diplomat might have tackled all these things in his stride but then he would not have to write dozens of school reports or juggle the finances for a new science block. John had worked fourteen-hour days – often well past midnight – for years but running a school from 40,000 feet in a Boeing 747 in a different time zone was stretching that concept of 'multi-tasking' to its limits.

With the benefit of hindsight, he might have made life a lot easier for himself and had a better relationship with the Australian and Kiwi media had he taken a year's sabbatical. It might also have ultimately taken a lot less of a toll upon his health.

But that was not the way John Kendall-Carpenter did things. He knew it would be tough but he somehow just kept going.

27

Now Is the Hour –
May 1987

The lilting song 'Now is the Hour' is a translation of an old Māori ballad '*Po Atarau*' and is often sung when men depart for home from rugby tours as indeed the Anzac troops had done on the way to fight and die at Gallipoli way back in the First World War.

On Friday 22 May 1987 that hour would at last arrive when the ball would be kicked off and the result of all that blood, sweat and tears from putting this major new venture together would at last come into being. Writing in the lead article in *Rugby World* that month, John expressed his hopes for the tournament and paid due thanks to his colleagues in Australia and New Zealand for getting the show on the road.

Despite everything he still remained true to the ideal of amateurism remaining at the heart and soul of the sport.

> Some people choose to regard this tournament as the 'first shot' at professionalism. I see it as the reverse; the proving ground for amateurism. In many respects it represents a condensed tour for the visiting nations, with a maximum duration of about six weeks, which is not excessive and which has allowed almost every player in contention for his national squad to afford the time required to take part.

Certainly, it was a great deal shorter than a full Lions tour, which in those days would involve being away for over four months. Not only this initial tournament, but two further World Cups would also be completed satisfactorily before professionalism became an established fact.

This first tournament was to comprise some sixteen national teams divided into four pools of four. Three of these pools would be contested in New Zealand and one in Australia after which the top two in each pool would progress to a knock-out quarter final. Next there would be two semi-finals in Australia culminating in a Final scheduled for 20 June in Auckland. This well-tried format has continued to this day with a 'last sixteen' round now added to deal with the increased number of participating nations.

The first group contained both England and Australia together with Japan and the United States and the matches were shared between the Concord Oval in Sydney and the Ballymore stadium in Brisbane. Both were very modest venues by today's standards and probably reflected a certain lack of confidence on the part of the Australian organisers who feared the prospect of televising matches in front of tiers of empty seats.

The second pool involved Wales, Ireland, Canada and Tonga and were spread around no fewer than six different venues right across New Zealand. Apart from Wellington and one match over in Australia, these were awarded to provincial towns and cities with relatively small venues such as Dunedin and Invercargill in the far South and Napier and Palmerston North on the North Island. Here a political decision had clearly been made to allow as many New Zealanders as possible to see at least some of the action first hand at their local rugby grounds.

The third pool had New Zealand playing their three matches at the three largest Test Match stadiums at Eden Park in Auckland, Athletic Park in Wellington and Lancaster Park in Christchurch. Other games were at Dunedin and at Hamilton in Waikato with the group being completed by Argentina, Fiji and Italy.

The Final pool was comprised of France, Scotland, Romania and Zimbabwe and again involved all the four old Test venues in Auckland, Wellington, Dunedin and Christchurch.

Just as everything was about to start, there was yet another political upheaval when there was a military coup in Fiji and for several days it was uncertain whether their team would actually turn up. Frantic contingency plans were being made to invite Western Samoa in their place who themselves were no doubt nursing a considerable grievance at having not being invited in the first place. As it turned out the Fijians did manage to arrive a few days later than planned and then gave a good account of themselves by defeating the Argentinians and only losing narrowly to Italy.

On the face of it, and barring major upsets, the eight IRB countries should have all progressed serenely into the quarter-finals with Wales v Ireland, England v Australia and France v Scotland being the hardest to call. After that, things were likely to get a lot more competitive.

John's own country of England were going through a difficult period with the team transitioning from the old era under Bill Beaumont to the next successful one under Will Carling. They were currently led by a Yorkshireman named Mike Harrison, nicknamed 'Burglar Bill' on account of him scoring a number of intercepted tries. He was a talented player but his main problem in communicating with his team was that he was stuck out on the wing in an era before such players were expected to get more involved, come in and hurl themselves into breakdowns and tackle prop forwards as is the case today. The team included several young men on their way up, such as Rob Andrew, Brian Moore, Jonathan Webb, Wade Dooley and Dean Richards, but their particular glory days all lay in the future. Perhaps England's only current star performer was the Headingley flanker Peter Winterbottom.

The Scots included the famous Hastings brothers – Gavin and Scott – plus a fine hooker in Colin Deans, two top-rank flankers in John Jeffrey and Finlay Calder plus a more than adequate half-back partnership of Rutherford and Laidlaw. However, as has so often been the case, they did not have the necessary strength in depth to be able to field an entire squad capable of going all the way to the final stages.

For their part the Irish had seen their exciting 1985 team (which had topped the Five Nations) crumble before their eyes to finish bottom in the season just completed and morale had inevitably suffered seriously as a result. Their impressive captain, Donal Lenihan, had a few very good, experienced players around him but some were probably past their best and several others not quite the 'real deal' when it came to the final stages of the competition.

Curiously, despite producing dozens of magnificent players and frequently having their provincial teams sweep the board in European competitions, Ireland have somehow yet to do themselves full justice after no fewer than nine World Cups having taken place.

The big Home Nations' hope would probably have been Wales and they had some top-flight men to call upon such as Jonathan Davies and Rob Jones at half-back plus Ieuan Evans and the big boot of Paul Thorburn in the backs. But, with the honourable exception of Bob Norster, the pack lacked the experience of several Welsh teams of the immediate past. They were to dispose of a poor England team in the quarter-finals and as such could rightfully claim to have given the best – or perhaps least bad – performance by any of the 'Home' nations.

Since its inception, the World Cup has grown and flourished to take its rightful place as the third biggest international sporting event behind only the FIFA World Cup and the Olympic Games. It is now customary for it to be opened – and the winning trophy presented – by a head of state such as King Charles or the Emperor of Japan. Back in 1987 this was far from the case and John was prevailed upon to perform the opening speech with Albert Ferrasse presenting the trophy after the Final.

John had been on the end of plenty of sniping from all directions but, now that it was actually about to take place, people had belatedly realised that it would arguably never have happened without him. Indeed, if Shehadie and Littlejohn were the parents of the World Cup, John was probably the midwife who had done more than anyone else to finally deliver the baby. As it is hardly appropriate to think of a strapping macho male like John as a 'midwife' we shall content ourselves with viewing him as the 'Godfather' of the new competition.

When he stood up at Eden Park in Auckland to open the tournament it was all just a bit underwhelming. For some reason best known to the local organisers the opening match featuring the All Blacks took place on a Friday afternoon and a thin drizzle fell across the stadium, which was noticeably less than full. The ceremony included a gaggle of go-go dancers incongruously mixed in with music by Strauss and wailing bagpipes. Then the old All Blacks flanker Waka Nathan trotted around the pitch clutching a rugby ball which he rather self-consciously handed over to John. As a first step into the brave new world of razzmatazz it was all just a wee bit half-hearted.

John's opening speech then rambled on for a couple of minutes longer than the allotted time, which caused a fair amount of chaos in terms of the planned commercial break on the television channels. This cannot have endeared him to the various sponsors and advertisers but there was not much that they could do about it.

Once it all got going, the British teams all performed poorly with England going out meekly to Wales in the quarter-finals only for the Welsh in turn to be massacred by the All Blacks in the semis by eight tries to one. The All Blacks had already disposed of Scotland whilst the Irish had also gone under to the Wallabies. In terms of the Southern Hemisphere versus the 'Home Nations' it had been an embarrassing whitewash.

When it came to the gulf between South and North one has to defer to the great Gerald Davies – surely one of the finest Welsh backs in the history of the game – when he was to write about that semi-final and his country's fate in his *History of the World Cup* some sixteen years later.

New Zealand demonstrated the special requirements of power, discipline and efficiency. There was no imaginative adventure here. Yet in raw strength, disciplined rhythm and sheer simplicity of execution there was a kind of beauty. This was no contest between equally matched teams. There was a vast gulf, a veritable Grand Canyon, which separated them. The All Blacks laid Wales on a slab and, coldly and dispassionately, dissected its battered and bruised body.

Coming from a proud Welshman who, as a member of the 1971 Lions had defeated the All Blacks in their own back yard, this must have been a painful paragraph to have written. One can only speculate that had it been England, Ireland or Scotland out there it might have been just as bad – if not even worse.

The big revelation from Europe was the French who, having started with a nervy draw with the Scots in Christchurch, turned on the style as only they can. Their 30-24 semi-final triumph over Australia was an absolute rugby classic with Serge Blanco scoring a magnificent try which can still be enjoyed on YouTube today.

Unfortunately, they had rather emptied the tank by the time the Final itself took place and New Zealand predictably ran out as the comfortable first winners. The IRFB chairman, Albert Ferrasse, swallowing his understandable disappointment at his own country's defeat, presented the glittering new Cup to the All Blacks' poster boy scrum-half and captain David Kirk, and it was smiles and handshakes all round. Perhaps the Springboks might somehow have upset the party had they not been debarred or things might have happened differently if the New Zealanders had suspended all those Cavaliers who had defied the authorities by playing in South Africa. We shall never know.

The fact remained that the hosts New Zealand were the best team in the competition by some distance and the very first tournament had gone through without any major hitches. The All Blacks had paraded the best winger in the world in John Kirwan who had even outshone the highly talented and super-confident David Campese. They were the two best wingers around for a few more years until a new face announced himself to the world.

His name was of course Jonah Lomu.

28

Lessons Learned

The players, media and supporters had all departed back to their homes, families and clubs and it was now time to undertake a cold, objective review of what had gone well and what still needed some drastic rethinking.

It should be borne in mind that there was absolutely no guarantee that there would ever be a second tournament and had it failed it would have been just a 'one-off' accompanied by a lot of 'I told you so's' from every Doubting Thomas sitting on the sidelines.

From a purely rugby point of view, it should certainly have been considered a great success. It was inevitable that there should be some very one-sided games in the preliminary rounds when some of the relative minnows were pitched against teams like the Wallabies and All Blacks. The rugby had not become particularly negative nor overly-defensive and there had not been any significant increase in foul play. There had been one sour note in the New Zealand v Wales semi-final when Welsh lock Huw Richards had been sent off by the Australian referee whilst Buck Shelford, who had clearly punched Richards, was allowed to stay on the pitch and thereafter take his place in the Final – as did the same referee a mere six days later. Something did not feel quite right there.

Despite this unfortunate episode, the ability to use entirely neutral referees and insist upon a more consistent interpretation of the Laws of the game had generally worked well and set the standard for the future.

Some new stars like Sean Fitzpatrick and John Kirwan had emerged. Perhaps more importantly a number who had already been around for three or four years such as Phillipe Sella, Michael Lynagh, Serge Blanco and David Campese were now being seen and appreciated by a far wider world audience than would otherwise have been the case. This could only do the sport of Rugby Union a power of good.

There was no getting away from that brutal fact that the four Home Unions had all failed to make any great impression with Wales being the only one to even reach a semi-final. Indeed they had only achieved this by overcoming a disappointingly lacklustre England. The message was blindingly obvious: if a team was sent out a bit half-heartedly by their own Union, they were on a hiding to nothing. A World Cup staged in Europe held out the possibility of them doing very much better but administrators, players, coaches, media and the paying public were all going to have to take the competition much more seriously.

Attendances were just about passable in New Zealand but were often disappointing in Australia. Despite all the marketing efforts, the crowd at that classic Australia v France semi-final in Sydney had only been 18,000. The third place play-off between Australia and Wales had been tucked away in rural Rotorua, a beautiful place if you like hot springs but hardly the centre of the rugby universe.

On the commercial and marketing side considerable efforts had been made in a ridiculously short time. West Nally had struggled and in fact went into temporary liquidation before bouncing back later. In particular the broadcasting side needed a lot of attention. Back in the UK the BBC had been rather lukewarm on the entire venture and Murdoch's SKY SPORT did not appear on the scene for another eleven years. The unavoidable situation in that any live matches would have to be screened in the early morning in Europe was an obvious issue but, by the same token, any European-based competition would create similar timing problems for audiences in Australasia. With the exception of Japan, coverage around the world had indeed been a bit hit-and-miss, but it still represented a big step forward over what had been available before. Furthermore, it was a lot clearer as to how it could be further improved in the future.

The big issue was going to be Finance. The 1987 tournament was widely feared to be heading for a big loss or at the very best a 'break even' situation and taxation of profits had not as yet been a major issue. The next one – and it was soon apparent that there would indeed *be* a next one – was to take place in Europe with the epicentre logically being London. This would undoubtedly become a much more elaborate affair and the European rugby unions would all now be looking to receive a healthy income stream from the expected profits.

The various Home Unions had a particular need to raise additional funds and that was the increasingly urgent requirement to update their stadiums. In 1985 football had suffered two disasters – a fire at Bradford City and a collapsed wall at the Heysel stadium in Brussels – each leading to multiple deaths. Then, just two years before the 1991 World Cup was to take place, a third one had led to an appalling loss of life at Hillsborough in Sheffield. Although football was the primary concern, any government's severe limits on crowd sizes could potentially make big rugby matches financially non-viable as well.

Both Wales and France had already begun to address the issue in the early 1970s. The renovation of the old Arms Park into what was then to become known as the National Stadium in Cardiff had only been a partial solution but was a step in the right direction. As for the French, the rebuilt modern Parc des Princes in the centre of Paris had at last replaced the rickety old hulk that was the Stade Colombes. However, Murrayfield, Lansdowne Road and particularly Twickenham were all in a sorry state.

Apart from having replaced the old propped terracing behind the south end with a modern double-decker cantilevered stand, Twickenham with its three dark and forbidding Archibald Leitch stands looked almost exactly the same as it had done when John was playing. Indeed, it had actually remained largely untouched since the early 1930s. The roofs had old-fashioned upright supports which interfered with spectators' view of play, the stairways were dangerous, the toilets stank and there were not even any floodlights.

The RFU had appointed a new secretary in Dudley Wood who, as John had already discovered, would have the primary task of master-minding the complete rebuilding of Twickenham. Wood had quickly realised that he had a big job on his hands. Having come from a senior job at ICI, he was somewhat taken aback by just how backward much of the administration continued to be.

> When I first arrived, I was appalled to discover that the RFU's telephone number was ex-directory.

Another couple of insights were provided by Jules Boardman, who was then the London-based head honcho for Ticketmaster.

> When I first went to Twickenham to talk about ticketing strategy, I was amazed to discover that some dear old boy was keeping all the international tickets in bundles stashed into ancient wooden pigeon holes. I could hardly believe my eyes.

On a further occasion he called Twickenham to enquire about their policy regarding credit card sales to be blithely told by the chap answering the phone,

> Could you call back later please as Doris is the only one who understands about the card machine and she's in the loo.

Wood and his counterparts would soon start to sort out this kind of nonsense and start modernising things but to do that they were going to need money – and lots of it.

The world's political wheels were also turning very quickly. There had been a spectacular thawing of relationships between the West and the Soviet Union characterised by Mr Gorbachev's dual policies of *glasnost* and *perestroika*. Indeed, before the 1991 World Cup kicked off the entire communist bloc had imploded upon itself. The Berlin Wall had come down and the people of rugby-loving Romania and Georgia would now appear to be heading for a very different and hopefully much freer way of life.

Down in South Africa things were just beginning to stir as well. Hard-line President P. W. Botha had suffered a stroke and was replaced by the much more amenable and internationally aware F. W. De Klerk. John had met Botha on an earlier visit to South Africa and had teased the notoriously grumpy – his media nickname of 'Die Groot Krokodil' (The Great Crocodile) was apparently not misplaced – white supremacist by remarking, 'Send one of your young lads over to my school Mr Botha and I'll make a man of him.'

The old crocodile failed to be amused and cut him dead the next time their paths crossed, which must have allowed John to have had a quiet chuckle to himself.

Be that as it may, Nelson Mandela had actually been transferred from the notorious Robben Island prison to the mainland during the last months of Botha's regime. In 1988 he had then been allowed to live in relative comfort under house arrest by the new president. Hopes were just beginning to stir that a more liberal regime might somehow be on the distant horizon. Nevertheless, for the time being, there was still no prospect whatsoever of the Springboks competing in any World Cup occurring as soon as 1991. However, John retained a level of contact as, even then, hopes were cherished that 1995 might yet provide some sort of opportunity.

In summary, there was still a massive amount of work to be done with regard to improving media coverage, corporate sponsorship and financial management but John and his colleagues had passed their initial test. Despite all the barbs and criticisms, the crushing schedule of flying hours and the ambivalence of many, the concept of a World Cup – held every four years between the Olympics and the FIFA World Cup – was here to stay.

The baby had been delivered successfully.

29

1991 Will Soon Be Here

Following the 1987 World Cup, it had been confirmed that John would be continuing in his leadership position and, having by then reached the age of sixty-two, he might have been expected to be looking forward to retiring early from his headmastership at Wellington and thus being able to devote his entire energies to the forthcoming World Cup. That again was not the Kendall-Carpenter way and for the time being the dual pressures would continue to be just as relentless. This was particularly so as a major project was getting underway back at the school with the construction of that new modern science block.

As soon as any venture like a World Cup begins to make a profit the next big question is how best to hold on to it and be able to use it for the greater good of the sport and the organisations concerned. Hence John's hours and energies were now going to have to switch away from a frantic political merry-go-round to focus upon all the complexities of corporate taxation.

Accountants have a unique ability to make figures appear to be whatever you want them to be and there was a rather opaque query over whether the 1987 competition had somehow made a small profit or had actually run at a loss. There was now to be a change of the accounting firm for the next World Cup and over on the promotional side West Nally were being replaced by a rival named CPMA, the letter 'M' denoting the presence on its Board of Cliff Morgan, old Welsh fly-half and contemporary of John.

Happily, in 1986 a new member of the IRFB had arrived just before the initial World Cup with a highly experienced financial brain from France named Marcel Martin. He had been deeply involved in international accounting during a long career in the oil industry and, having received his MBA in the USA, spoke fluent English. He would come to play an important role in making that initial World Cup successful, not only from a rugby point of view, but into it later becoming a very lucrative undertaking as well.

Martin had immediately recognised that, now that the IRFB had funds and was embarking upon significant commercial contracts, it could no longer continue to operate on the old committee basis, especially if they were hopefully going to make substantial profits. Thus, even before the 1987 tournament, the organisation had been split into two entities.

The first continued to run the structure, fixtures, referees, rules, etc. whilst that new entity called Rugby World Cup (Pty Ltd) was set up to operate all the commercial undertakings and was registered in Australia. This ensured that whatever money was made would not be hoovered up by the taxman. John had acted as chairman for both organisations and was well aware that once the tournament moved to being run out of the UK that the issues of taxation would become infinitely more complex, especially as three separate governments in London, Paris and Dublin would then be involved. To this could be added the fact that everyone was by then confident that this time a handsome profit would indeed be forthcoming.

Compared to the mere twenty-three-month lead-up to 1987, the four-year gap until the next World Cup might have seemed relatively luxurious, but this was certainly not going to be the case. The Home Countries had at last taken on board the fact that this was now the ultimate yardstick as to who could legitimately claim to be 'World Champions' and any lingering opposition to the competition taking place had by then all but vanished.

England in particular began to take a longer-term view of trying to build a squad of players who would come to the next World Cup not only knowing one another's personalities, playing strengths and weaknesses but who would also arrive for the opening match having each accumulated at least twenty 'caps' along the way. Gone at last were the days when an almost unknown player might shine in a Trial or an inter-regional match and then be tossed into the team by a whimsical selection committee to see if he would sink or swim.

Wales, Scotland and Ireland, with much smaller pools of players to draw upon, had often turned this apparent handicap to their advantage by the fact that their best players virtually picked themselves and as a result could usually look forward to longer international careers than their English counterparts. This was especially pertinent in the heat of a tight match when a less-experienced man, however talented, might make a fatal error or communication failure at a crucial moment and there had been plenty of examples of these over the past couple of decades.

Immediately after the 1987 team had returned home, the RFU had recruited a Yorkshireman named Geoff Cooke as chief coach and he had clearly set out upon a course of building an experienced squad. He soon appointed a very young but charismatic captain in Will Carling and, just as importantly, stuck with him even after a few disappointing defeats.

Similarly, he introduced a few new players such as lock Paul Ackford, back row man Mike Teague, prop Jeff Probyn plus full-back Jonathan Webb (one of England's few successes among the new boys in 1987) and continued to persevere with them despite legitimate claims from many others. Even when his team were denied Grand Slams through disappointing defeats by small margins both at Cardiff in 1989 and memorably at Murrayfield a year later, he refused to panic and continued to patiently build his squad.

During the interim between the first two World Cups, the Lions had embarked upon their first ever full tour of Australia and had come home with a

2-1 series victory. This helped to give all the Home Nations the feeling that with the next tournament being held in Europe they all had at least a sporting chance.

It was agreed that, whilst the Final would be held at Twickenham, all five European nations would host at least some of the matches which would not only feature the five national stadiums but also, as in 1987, include a series of provincial venues. It was a noble concept but it must be conceded that some of the chosen venues such as Pontypridd, Otley and Brive were still going to present a rather folksy image to any global TV audience.

There would once again be four groups of four based upon England, France and Wales with Scotland and Ireland co-hosting one of the groups. The same teams would be invited to compete with the sole exception of Western Samoa replacing Tonga. So far so good, but the big issue facing John and his colleagues was how this was going to be sold to sponsors, the media and now, being largely based in the United Kingdom, the big question of how could it steer its way around all those rocks and depredations of the Inland Revenue?

All corporations of any sophistication go to considerable lengths to structure themselves in a way which legitimately minimises the amount of tax they have to pay. Today we are acutely conscious of how some of the IT giants, oil companies, major pharmaceutical corporations and others have managed to refine this art to a level which some might consider almost obscene.

John and the rest of the organisers were anxious not to venture into the muddy waters of anything which could be construed by any hostile media as 'tax evasion' but were, at the same time, acutely conscious that a lot of rugby organisations around the world were relying upon what they hoped would be a financial lifeline.

After the 1987 tournament, not only were West Nally out of the picture, but the global accountants Ernst and Young were also replaced by a smaller, specialist UK-based firm named Neville-Russell.

Time does not permit delving too deeply into all the complex financial structuring, but there was no doubt in the minds of both John and Keith Rowlands that if the dream of future tournaments and fulfilling the vision of helping to fund the world's rugby 'minnows' was to succeed, the retention of profits was an absolute must. In all of this John would clearly have relied heavily upon the advice of his taxation experts.

Aware of the potential threat posed by the UK Inland Revenue, Albert Ferrasse predictably offered to base all the financial operations in France where playing hare and hounds with the tax authorities is a national pastime. Irishman Ronnie Dawson also made a similar offer to set something up in Shannon, which has a tax status not unlike Delaware in the USA. The UK countries were nevertheless determined that this should all be controlled within Britain itself but would set up a suitable structure to minimise the tax liabilities.

Accordingly, a Trust was set up with Barclays in the Isle of Man, which also has a well-recognised tax exemption status. At the same time a second (Dutch) company named Rugby World Cup (Licensing) BV was set up based in Rotterdam. The Trust was to accumulate and distribute all the surplus profits. Being run by external Trustees, it had the added benefit that no individual nation's rugby men would be able to grab more than their due share. Other countries, including the Americans, have traditionally always suspected the English of somehow being up to something.

This reputedly prompted the remark (once used in the past to describe wartime relationships between Britain and the USA) which has been attributed to both John and Dudley Wood to the effect that,

> The relationship between the English and the Welsh is based upon trust and understanding. They don't trust us and we don't understand them.

In recent years this structure has been modified on more than one occasion and additional elements added as required. As the competition has expanded and developed (the sums involved have escalated from a few million dollars in the early days to 2019 in Japan when it could be computed in billions), so have the financial structuring imperatives grown accordingly.

Given the fact that the 1991 tournament was to be held in Europe, John might have expected the demand for constant long-distance travel to be eased. If so, he was to be disappointed as the constant merry-go-round and absence from Wellington School continued unabated. His dutiful secretary Jackie Waters would still be dealing with constant streams of paper pouring off the fax machine.

He would still need to meet his Australian and New Zealander counterparts – sometimes in Singapore (and on one occasion in Moscow) – and the competing countries would all still need to be visited and reassured. Meetings were originally held in the RFU's old haunt of the East India Club and then moved to a small building formerly used by Wood's RFU predecessor Bob Weighill at Twickenham. Both John and his Welsh counterparts (Rowlands and ex-coach Ray Williams) would have preferred a base in Bristol which was much more accessible for all of them and had their eyes on a building which had once been owned by Harveys – of Bristol Cream sherry fame.

Thus, a new aspect of John's work was having to visit repeatedly both Rotterdam and the Isle of Man. His principal contact from Neville-Russell was a partner named Peter Hyatt. He recalled,

> We seemed to be constantly on little planes buzzing between these two places and London. I was very rarely able to sit beside him as he would inevitably commandeer two seats with a massive pile of papers stacked up on the seat next to him. I soon realised these were detailed school reports and testimonials for pupils applying to universities plus all the administrative and financial bumph that was part and parcel of life back at Wellington School. That pressure on two fronts continued to be relentless.

Before any organisation can become overly concerned about holding onto its income it naturally has to make it in the first place. This would be forthcoming through four different income streams. Ticketing for the various matches, television and other broadcasting rights, sponsorship deals and, for the first time, merchandise ranging from replica shirts to glossy magazines to woolly toys, rugby balls on key rings and so on.

One major challenge for John was that each country seemed to insist on administratively doing their own thing. Ticketing was a good example of this. Partially prompted by the Hillsborough disaster, the English authorities were looking at all ways of gaining better control of entrance to stadiums and who exactly went where. An up-and-coming company called SYNCHRO had already introduced computerised ticketing into both Arsenal and Tottenham Hotspur football clubs and were now expanding this rapidly across the various clubs in what was then still called the First Division.

This became the method adopted not only by Dudley Wood and his staff at Twickenham but also at Gloucester and even little Otley, although the folks at Leicester continued to want to do their own thing. Before long all those days of sheaves of tickets crammed into wooden pigeon holes were gone forever.

Television rights were again open to bids. Although the TV contracts were not finalised until after John's untimely death in May 1990, the UK rights ended up with ITV and so the main commentator for the tournament was the ex-Wales and British Lions flanker John Taylor rather than the BBC and Nigel Starmer-Smith. ITV got good value from their investment as a reported thirteen million UK viewers tuned in for the Final, thus creating the then highest ever rugby television audience to date. This has created a long association between the World Cup and ITV sport. Despite the time difference, the largest Australian night time TV audience in history also sat up to watch the Wallabies defeat England.

As for sponsors, the number seemed to proliferate to the extent that it is hard to see what they actually got from it. Both Mazda and Rank Xerox continued from 1987 but when ITV sport produced a glossy official World Cup guide, they appeared to be swamped out by a whole mish-mash of advertisers and sponsors which now included several (competing) brands of whisky, to motor cars, soups, building societies, airlines, sports kit manufacturers plus some products that few people would even have recognised. Since those days the branding has been streamlined to a small number of major corporations who – for very large sums of money – get naming rights, television and revolving pitch-side advertisements, interview access to players and coaches, etc.

John would have had little directly to do with all this and whether he would have approved of either the scattergun approach or indeed all the more recent rampant commercialism itself is unlikely.

It was tough enough for him just to get five different nations to work together.

30

Goodbye Too Soon

On his long flight back from that initial World Cup in 1987 one imagines that John would have taken stock of his situation. He could have taken immense satisfaction in what had been achieved, although he would have been less than human had he not been affected by all the barbs and often personal criticism he had suffered along the way. Despite this he was soon to be elected as chairman of the IRFB which was then the ultimate position in World Rugby.

He would perhaps also have recognised that his frantic lifestyle was bound to have taken its toll. Maybe not – but he was certainly not to know that he had less than three years left to live. His father had survived to a ripe old age and, although he had suffered that heart attack following his unhappy sojourn at Eastbourne, he had recovered well and his relentless schedule of multi-tasking and working long hours far into the night had continued unabated.

Given his achievements and lofty positions both in rugby and headmastership, he lived in a surprisingly modest way. He loved to get a bargain and often bought up lots of things from army surplus. Whatever money he did have largely went towards his family's education. When travelling in the UK he also thought nothing of spending the night in the back of his trusty VW camper van in a convenient layby rather than booking into a hotel as just about anyone else would have done. He would also retire to it in order to do his correspondence in relative peace and quiet.

Another little episode from a few years previously illustrates both his engaging generosity and kindness but also a certain 'other-worldliness' when it came down to making detailed arrangements. The RFU had appointed an ex-England full-back named Don Rutherford as its first paid Technical Director, a somewhat vague title which did not include coaching the England team. He and his wife Sue lived in a small grace-and-favour house within the bounds of Twickenham. John kindly offered them the use of the family house for a short holiday in Cornwall. They duly drove down to Penzance with their small children and were somewhat taken aback to discover that not only was the house unlocked but also that John's elderly father Tim was already temporarily staying there. He was just as taken aback as Don and Sue but John had clearly not seen any particular necessity to mention it to any of them.

John was by now in his early sixties, his hips continued to play him up badly but he was determined to take the World Cup to a much higher plane and knew that basing it in Europe would give him that chance. Thus, the merry-go-round of running a growing school and all those preparations for the next tournament never stopped spinning.

The fact that the future of the World Cup was no longer seriously in doubt had not removed those two ongoing bugbears which surrounded the IRFB and hence continued to pile pressure upon John. They were of course the slow – but by now clearly unstoppable – creep towards top players getting remunerated for playing and the still seemingly intractable issue of South Africa.

The first worry was largely centralised inside the corridors of power within the game itself and there was no doubt that the goalposts, with regard to expenses for lost time and inducements to go and play as a 'guest' in a foreign country, were shifting very rapidly. It was widely rumoured that the South African star Naas Botha was being offered $100,000 plus living expenses to play for a club in Italy and several famous All Blacks had already played overseas and clearly been richly rewarded for doing so. Some of them numbered among John's shrillest critics.

The IRFB, in which John played a very central role, had attempted to impose a twelve-week moratorium between a player arriving in another country and being allowed to play. This was easily circumvented simply because there was no way a man could be prevented from travelling wherever he so wished nor indeed how he might spend his leisure time once he had arrived.

Furthermore, individual unions could make reciprocal arrangements to get around this and the South Africans and many others were perfectly happy to co-operate with each other in order to do so. In addition, hundreds of young men from overseas, including university students, were playing at all levels in the UK and elsewhere, so there were exceptions and grey areas everywhere. The mandarins of the amateur game might have blown a fuse over all this but probably nobody else cared very much.

On the other hand, the question of South Africa and its place in world sport in general was a much wider issue. It caused not only a great deal of political pressure but also stirred up much deeply held passion among millions of people around the globe, most of whom had little or no interest in rugby. As far as vast swathes of people were concerned the continuation of any sporting links with South Africa was totally unacceptable. Athletics and cricket had cut off all sporting relationships long ago but rugby had continued to try to somehow reconcile itself to clinging onto a measure of contact long after everyone else had given up and treated the men in green and gold as sporting pariahs.

As an astute and educated man with his finger on the pulse of matters in South Africa, John perhaps understood before most of the protestors that the political tectonic plates were at last beginning to shift down in Pretoria. With the all-too-easy benefit of hindsight, we all now know that in 1989 F. W. De Klerk became first elected as leader of the Nationalist Party and a few months later succeeded P. W. Botha as president. We also now know that Nelson Mandela and many other activists were being freed from incarceration and that by 1992 South Africa had changed forever.

However back in 1988–89, when John was wrestling with the seemingly impossible issue of continued South African involvement in rugby, nobody could have imagined anything would change so profoundly and moreover quite so fast. After all, De Klerk had grown up both as a Nationalist politician and as a man steeped in the ways of apartheid. It was also known that Mandela was at first extremely wary of him and that Bishop Desmond Tutu apparently dismissed his election as 'Just musical chairs'.

All official tours involving South Africa had by then fizzled out with the last Lions tour having taken place way back in 1980, although England made a final and catastrophic (both in political and rugby terms) trip there in 1984. The Springboks had of course wisely stayed well away from the first World Cup but they were still discreetly courting unofficial tours by groups of individual high-profile players – quite a few of whom were likely to be tempted by the 'illicit' inducements on offer.

The IRFB had made life even more difficult for itself by continuing to include the South Africans in the governing body and furthermore electing a white ex-Springbok lock forward named Jan Pickard onto its powerful five-man Policy Committee. Quite a few knives were going to be plunged into the backs of those who had sanctioned this – none more so than John.

An added complication was that the South African Rugby Union was about to celebrate its centenary. As a historian, John would have been well aware of how Cornish and Welsh miners had gone out to seek their fortunes in the gold mines up on the Rand in the 1880s and had brought the game to the Transvaal with them. This in turn had been eagerly adopted by the tough Boer farmers as it was ideally suited to their values and temperaments and thus the game had flourished despite the tragedy of the two Boer Wars.

England, Scotland, Wales and Ireland had all celebrated their centenaries in recent years often with several individual South Africans participating as welcome guests. The Springboks naturally also wanted to celebrate in style with special matches and this gave John and the rest of the Policy Committee another major headache. They were to be damned if they agreed and would cause huge offence back in Pretoria if they refused.

Just to compound this, the English and Welsh rugby unions had recently accepted some government funding for local development officers, which in itself was a very positive step forward in terms of stimulating coaching. However, it now gave local government some influence with regard to how the game was conducted and they had already begun to make their presence felt. In Wales in particular, during the past few years, rugby-playing schoolmasters and local government officials had been refused pay or even leave of absence if it involved playing in South Africa.

An example of all this suppressed angst came bubbling up to the surface when John attended a meeting of the Welsh clubs at Port Talbot in early October 1989 which was reported in a sympathetic article in the *Sunday Telegraph* by one of rugby's most astute commentators, John Reason.

The Welsh clubs, meeting in Port Talbot on Friday night to debate the fraught question of playing links with South Africa, degenerated into little more than a witch-hunt of England's John Kendall-Carpenter and Wales's former International Board delegate Terry Vaux.

Kendall-Carpenter took it upon himself to repair the damage and Terry Vaux tried to help him. The Welsh representatives who have taken their places even took their attack on Kendall-Carpenter into the recent meeting of the Five Nations Committee.

This was not an isolated incident. John was a man who kept his own counsel but, given the level of bile once again being directed against him just for doing his best to reconcile an impossible situation, he must have wondered to himself just why he even bothered.

In view of all this he must have looked forward to his impending retirement from Wellington school the following summer when he could then concentrate on the World Cup for the next eighteen months and then begin to take on things which he could actually enjoy rather than having to endure constant carping.

He and Toby had by then divorced, the family were now fully grown up and some of them had by then married and daughter Diana was soon to produce the first of his grandchildren a mere four weeks before his untimely death. Eldest son Tim was working with Manchester Transport and Nick had recently left the Forces having seen active service in the Falklands (he saw action at Goose Green and in the taking of Mount Tumbledown) and Belize and was by then doing a postgraduate MBA at Cranfield. Elspeth was working overseas in a succession of third world countries whereas Diana was already living in New Zealand. Meanwhile Giles was a police officer based in Kent.

John could then have concentrated his energies entirely upon the World Cup and he and Keith Rowlands had by then already looked into basing the organising office in that Harvey's building in Bristol. This would have taken him back to the city where his teaching career had begun nearly thirty years before at Clifton. It is understood that John would probably have temporarily based himself there but no doubt contemplated returning to his beloved Cornwall in due course.

Accordingly, during the following spring the governors at Wellington School embarked on the difficult task of trying to find someone to fill his very considerable shoes. It proved to be anything but a smooth process due to the fact that, having decided upon a particular candidate and with their job offer accepted, it then emerged that the man in question had been involved in a scandal at a previous school. News of this naturally soon leaked out and, despite the job offer being rescinded, worried parents were already contacting the office threatening to remove their daughters from the school.

John should have been looking forward to his retirement and concentrating fully upon arrangements for the 1991 World Cup. However, he now had a thoroughly distasteful moral issue dumped onto his plate as well. For all that he had appeared reasonably fit and healthy, he was also suffering by then from swollen feet largely brought about by his constant long-distance aeroplane flights.

By late May 1990 his retirement celebrations were only a matter of days away. A couple of weeks before his first grandchild had been born in New

Zealand and, although he was destined never to see any of his eventual six grandchildren, he would proudly show off the photographs of the new baby to everyone who came into his office. All of his daughter Diana's three sons have somehow inherited the sporting gene – including that innate ability to read a game – from the famous grandfather they were destined never to meet.

He was already well into his final term at Wellington and on the night of 23/24 May worked on as usual until the early hours before retiring to bed. During the night he died suddenly of a heart attack.

His then deputy, Alan Rogers (who was soon to be appointed as the new permanent headmaster), took an early call at home and by breakfast time the entire school was in a profound state of shock. Whilst many people were fully aware of how much pressure John had allowed himself to be under, this was a complete 'bolt from the blue'. Being still based in the UK, Giles was the first to arrive to be followed by the rest of the family on the next available flights.

John's colleague on the IRFB, Keith Rowlands, immediately called Alan and then descended on Wellington School and took away all his World Cup files and correspondence. This was probably both necessary and unavoidable but, as he has also since died, much fascinating history has now vanished forever.

An elaborate retirement celebration had been planned which included, among other things, a commissioned painting of the school, a beautiful engraved glass bowl and numerous other dinners, presentations and events. All these of course had to be cancelled and funeral arrangements hurriedly made in their place. Messages of condolence poured in from all over the world of rugby, other sporting bodies, many from Cornwall and all the multitude of various activities he had undertaken.

Most people have a funeral and perhaps a memorial service. John had five. His actual burial took place for close friends and family in the little parish church in the village of Gulval, which lies just a mile outside of Penzance. That burial was to be followed by a packed memorial service in Truro Cathedral where his lifelong friend Harvey Richards gave a moving eulogy. Then there was another back at Wellington School and a further one organised by the Rugby Union in London.

Finally, there was to be yet one more, which was out in New Zealand, arranged by the NZRFU probably at the prompting of Dick Littlejohn and Bob Stuart, where both daughters and later Giles were to make their homes.

The new science block was formally opened by Tim at the next Speech Day with the rest of the family in attendance. It was dedicated as the John Kendall-Carpenter Science Centre which has since prompted hundreds of girls and boys to pursue scientific careers.

The little boy with the high-pitched voice had come a very long way in a life, which had been ended so suddenly and cruelly when he still had so much to look forward to. Quite a few eminent rugby players have racked up many achievements outside of the sport in business, politics and the arts. One such was Sir Tony O'Reilly, the flame-haired Irish star who rose to become the head of Heinz, as well as a newspaper magnate, a doctor of law, a gifted raconteur and much besides. O'Reilly was once described by no less than Henry Kissinger as a 'true Renaissance man' and this could surely have been applied to John as well.

Two years after his death a 'John Kendall-Carpenter Memorial Fund' was set up by some of his friends with the aim of providing grants to aspiring young boys and girls predominantly in Cornwall. The accent was placed upon sporting excellence and it continued to help ambitious youngsters for over twenty years.

Sadly, John was destined never to be knighted although, had he been spared just a few more years, that particular honour might well have been bestowed upon him. He was posthumously inducted into world rugby's hall of fame – the supreme honour which the sport can bestow – but he had of course already been honoured by the Gorsedd in Cornwall several years before.

However, just a couple of years before his death he was summoned to Buckingham Palace to receive the CBE. His hectic latter life could perhaps be summed up by his brief exchange with the Queen. She was always very well briefed about everyone she met but, when he was introduced, her officials had concentrated upon his rugby achievements.

'I thought you were the headmaster of a large school Mr Kendall-Carpenter?'
'Well, your Majesty I am ... in my spare time.'

That was the life he had chosen to lead.

But the very last word should probably be a nod back to the sport that John clearly loved so much. Rugby football has always been a fierce and occasionally violent contest but, come the final whistle, it has an almost unique capacity to draw old teammates – and indeed old foes – together into a deep and lasting bond. This is probably only mirrored by the emotions of old miners and trawlermen or even army comrades who have faced danger, fought – and perhaps even died – alongside one another.

For years afterwards, whenever Dick Littlejohn travelled to the UK from his home in New Zealand, he would take the train from London for the seven-hour journey down to Penzance. He would then walk out to Gulval to sit quietly by his old friend's grave. He would always drink down a Steinlager and then leave a bottle for John nestling by the graveside. Rugby's capacity to engender those deep and lasting friendships can never be overstated. Sometimes they even last forever.

APPENDIX

The Big Matches

ENGLAND

Feb 12 1949 – **IRELAND** – Dublin – Lost 5-14
Ireland: G. W. Norton, M. F. Lane, T. J. Gavin, W. D. McKee, B. O'Hanlon, J. W. Kyle, E. Strathdee, A. A. McConnell, K. D. Mullen (capt), T. Clifford, J. E. Nelson, C. P. Callan, J. W. McKay, D. J. O'Brien, J. S. McCarthy.
Scorers: T. O'Hanlon McKee, C. Norton, P. Norton 2
England: W. B. Holmes, D. W. Swarbrick, C. B. van Ryneveld, L. B. Cannell, R. D. Kennedy, N. M. Hall (capt), G. R. Rimmer, T. W. Price, A. P. Henderson, M. J. Berridge, G. R. D'A. Hosking, J. T. George, D. B. Vaughan, J. MacG. Kendall-Carpenter, V. G. Roberts.
Scorers: T. van Ryneveld, C. Holmes
Referee: R. A. Beattie (Scotland)

Feb 26 1949 – **FRANCE** – Twickenham – Won 8-3
England: W. B. Holmes, R. H. Guest, C. B. van Ryneveld, L. B. Cannell, R. D. Kennedy, I. Preece (capt), W. K. T. Moore, T. W. Price, J. H. Steeds, J. MacG. Kendall-Carpenter, G. R. D'A. Hosking. J. R. C. Matthews, B. H. Travers, D. B. Vaughan, V. G. Roberts.
Scorers: T. Cannell, C. Holmes, D. G. Preece
France: A. J. Alvarez, M. Pomathios, P. Dizabo, R. Dutrain, J. Lassegue, J. Pilon, Y. R. Bergougnan, L. Caron, M. Jol, E. Buzy, A. Moga, R. Soro, J. Prat, G. Basquet (capt), J. Matheu.
Scorer: D. G. Alvarez
Referee: T. Jones (Wales)

Mar 19 1949 – **SCOTLAND** – Twickenham – Won 19-3
England: W. B. Holmes, R. H. Guest, C. B. van Ryneveld, L. B. Cannell, R. D. Kennedy, I. Preece (capt), W. K. T. Moore, T. W. Price, J. H. Steeds, J. MacG. Kendall-Carpenter, G. R. D'A. Hosking, J. R. C. Matthews, B. H. Travers, D. B. Vaughan, V. G. Roberts.
Scorers: T. van Ryneveld 2, Guest Hosking Kennedy, C. Travers 2
Scotland: I. J. M. Lumsden, T. G. H. Jackson, L. G. Gloag, D. P. Hepburn, D. W. C. Smith, C. R. Bruce, W. D. Allardice, S. Coltman, J. A. R. McPhail,

S. T. H. Wright, L. A. Currie, G. A. Wilson, D. H. Keller (capt), P. W. Kininmonth, W. I. D. Elliot.

Scorer: P. Wilson

Referee: N. H. Lambert (Ireland)

Jan 21 1950 – **WALES** – Twickenham – Lost 5-11

England: M. B. Hofmeyr, J. V. Smith, B. Boobbyer, L. B. Cannell, I. J. Botting, I. Preece (capt), G. Rimmer, J. MacG. Kendall-Carpenter, E. Evans, W. A. Holmes, H. A. Jones, G. R. D'A. Hosking, H. D. Small, D. B. Vaughan, J. J. Cain.

Scorers: T. Smith, C. Hofmeyr

Wales: B. L. Jones, K. J. Jones, M. C. Thomas, J. Matthews, T. J. Brewer, W. B. Cleaver, W. R. Willis, J. D. Robins, D. M. Davies, C. Davies, E. R. John, D. J. Hayward, W. R. Cale, J. A. Gwilliam (capt), R. T. Evans.

Scorers: T. Cale, C. Davies, C. B. L. Jones, P. B. L. Jones.

Referee: N. H. Lambert (Ireland)

Feb 11 1950 – **IRELAND** – Twickenham – Won 3-0

England: R. Uren, J. V. Smith, B. Boobbyer, L. B. Cannell, I. J. Botting, I. Preece (capt), W. K. T. Moore, J. MacG. Kendall-Carpenter, J. H. Steeds, W. A. Holmes, H. A. Jones, J. R. C. Matthews, H. D. Small, S. J. Adkins, V. G. Roberts.

Scorer: T. Roberts

Ireland: G. W. Norton, M. F. Lane, G. C. Phipps, W. D. McKee, L. Crowe, J. W. Kyle, J. H. Burges, D. R. McKibbin, K. D. Mullen (capt), T. Clifford, J. E. Nelson, R. D. Agar, A. B. Curtis, D. J. O'Brien, J. W. McKay.

Referee: R. A. Beattie (Scotland)

Feb 25 1950 – **FRANCE** – Paris – Lost 3-6

France: G. Brun, M. Siman, P. Lauga, J. Merquey, F. Cazenave, J. Pilon. G. Dufau, R. Bienes, P. Pascalin, R. Ferrien, L. Aristouy, F. Bonnus, J. Prat, G. Basquet (capt), J. Matheu.

Scorers: T. Cazenave Pilon

England: M. B. Hofmeyr, J. V. Smith, B. Boobbyer, L. B. Cannell, J. P. Hyde, I. Preece (capt) W. K. T. Moore, J. MacG. Kendall-Carpenter, J. H. Steeds, W. A. Holmes, H. A. Jones, J. R. C. Matthews, H. D. Small, S. J. Adkins, V. G. Roberts.

Scorer: T. Smith

Referee: N. H. Lambert (Ireland)

Mar 18 1950 – **SCOTLAND** – Edinburgh – Lost 11-13

Scotland: T. Gray, D. M. Scott, D. A. Sloan, R. McDonald, C. W. Drummond, A. Cameron, A. W. Black, J. C. Dawson, J. G. Abercrombie, G. M. Budge, R. Gemmill, D. E. Muir, W. I. D. Elliot, P. W. Kininmonth (capt), H. Scott.

Scorers: T. Sloan 2, Abercrombie C. Gray 2

England: M. B. Hofmeyr, J. V. Smith, B. Boobbyer, L. B. Cannell, J. P. Hyde, I. Preece (capt), W. K. T. Moore, J. L. Baume, J. H. Steeds, W. A. Holmes, J. R. C. Matthews, S. J. Adkins, H. D. Small, J. MacG. Kendall-Carpenter, V. G. Roberts.

Scorers: T. Smith 2, C. Hofmeyr 2, P. Hofmeyr

Referee: M. J. Dowling (Ireland)

Feb 10 1951 – IRELAND – Dublin – Lost 0-3

Ireland: G. W. Norton, C. S. Griffin, N. J. Henderson, R. R. Chambers, W. H. J. Millar, J. W. Kyle, J. A. O'Meara, T. Clifford, K. D. Mullen (capt), J. H. Smith, J. E. Nelson, D. McKibbin, J. W. McKay, D. J. O'Brien, J. S. McCarthy.

Scorer: P. McKibbin

England: E. N. Hewitt, C. G. Woodruff, J. M. Williams, I. Preece, V. R. Tindall, E. M. P. Hardy, G. Rimmer, R. V. Stirling, E. Evans, W. A. Holmes, B. A. Neale, D. T. Wilkins, G. C. Rittson-Thomas, J. MacG. Kendall-Carpenter (capt), V. G. Roberts.

Referee: T. Jones (Wales)

Feb 24 1951 – FRANCE –Twickenham – Lost 3-11

England: E. N. Hewitt, C. G. Woodruff, B. Boobbyer, I. Preece, V. R. Tindall, E. M. P. Hardy, G. Rimmer, R. V. Stirling, E. Evans, W. A. Holmes, B. A. Neale, D. T. Wilkins, G. C. Rittson-Thomas, J. MacG. Kendall-Carpenter (capt), V. G. Roberts.

Scorer: T. Boobbyer

France: R. Arcalis, A. Porthault, G. Brun, G. Belletante, M. Pomathios, A. J. Alvarez, G. Dufau, R. Bernard, P. Pascalin, P. Bertrand, L. Mias, H. Foures, J. Prat, G. Basquet (capt), R. Bienes.

Scorers: T. Basquet, Prat, C. Prat, P. Prat

Referee: V. S. Llewellyn (Wales)

Mar 17 1951 – SCOTLAND – Twickenham – Won 5-3

England: W. G. Hook, C. G. Woodruff, J. M. Williams, A. C. Towell, V. R. Tindall, E. M. P. Hardy, D. W. Shuttleworth, R. V. Stirling, E. Evans, W. A. Holmes, B. A. Neale, D. T. Wilkins, D. F. White, J. MacG. Kendall-Carpenter (capt), V. G. Roberts.

Scorers: T. White, C. Hook

Scotland: T. Gray, K. J. Dalgliesh, D. A. Sloan, D. M. Scott, D. M. Rose, A. Cameron, I. A. Ross, J. C. Dawson, N. G. R. Mair, R. L. Wilson, H. M. Inglis, W. P. Black, W. I. D. Elliot, P. W. Kininmonth (capt), R. C. Taylor.

Scorer: T. Cameron

Referee: M. J. Dowling (Ireland)

Jan 5 1952 – SOUTH AFRICA – Twickenham – Lost 3-8

England: W. G. Hook J. E. Woodward, A. E. Agar, L. B. Cannell, C. E. Winn, N. M. Hall (capt), G. Rimmer, R. V. Stirling, E. Evans, W. A. Holmes, J. R. C. Matthews, D. T. Wilkins, A. O. Lewis, J. MacG. Kendall-Carpenter, D. F. White.

Scorer: T. Winn

South Africa: J. U. Buchler, P. Johnstone, R. A. M. van Schoor, M. T. Lategan, J. K. Ochse, J. D. Brewis, P. A. du Toit, A. C. Koch, W. H. Delport, H. P. J. Bekker, E. E. Dinkelmann, J. A. du Rand, S. P. Fry, H. S. V. Muller (capt), C. J. van Wyk.

Scorers: T. du Toit, C. Muller, P. Muller

Referee: W. C. W. Murdoch (Scotland)

Jan 19 1952 – **WALES** – Twickenham – Lost 6-8

England: W. G. Hook, J. E. Woodward, A. E. Agar, L. B. Cannell, C. E. Winn, N. M. Hall (capt), G. Rimmer, R. V. Stirling, E. Evans, E. E. Woodgate, J. R. C. Matthews, D. T. Wilkins, A. O. Lewis, J. MacG. Kendall-Carpenter, D. F. White.

Scorers: T. Agar Woodward

Wales: G. Williams, K. J. Jones, M. C. Thomas, A. G. Thomas, B. L. Jones, C. I. Morgan, W. R. Willis, W. O. Williams, D. M. Davies, D. J. Hayward, E. R. John, J. R. G. Stephens, A. Forward, J. A. Gwilliam (capt), L. Blyth.

Scorers: T. K. J. Jones 2, C. M. C. Thomas

Referee: N. H. Lambert (Ireland)

Mar 15 1952 – **SCOTLAND** – Edinburgh – Won 19-3

Scotland: N. W. Cameron, R. A. Gordon, I. F. Cordial, I. D. F. Coutts, T. Weatherstone, J. N. G. Davidson, A. F. Dorward (capt), J. C. Dawson, J. Fox, J. M. Inglis, J. Johnston, D. E. Muir, W. I. D. Elliot, J. P. Friebe, D. S. Gilbert-Smith.

Scorer: T. Johnston

England: P. J. Collins, J. E. Woodward, A. E. Agar, B. Boobbyer, C. E. Winn, N. M. Hall (capt), P. W. Sykes, R. V. Stirling, E. Evans, W. A. Holmes, J. R. C. Matthews, D. T. Wilkins, A. O. Lewis, J. MacG. Kendall-Carpenter, D. F. White.

Scorers: Evans, Kendall-Carpenter, Winn, Woodward, C. Hall 2, D. G. Agar

Referee: M. J. Dowling (Ireland)

Mar 29 1952 – **IRELAND** – Twickenham – Won 3-0

England: P. J. Collins, C. E. Winn, A. E. Agar, B. Boobbyer, R. C. Bazley, N. M. Hall (capt), P. W. Sykes, R. V. Stirling, E. Evans, W. A. Holmes, J. R. C. Matthews, D. T. Wilkins, A. O. Lewis, J. MacG. Kendall-Carpenter, D. F. White.

Scorer: T. Boobbyer

Ireland: J. G. M. W. Murphy, M. Hillary, N. J. Henderson, G. C. Phipps, N. Bailey, J. W. Kyle, J. A. O'Meara, W. A. O'Neill, R. J. Roe, J. H. Smith, P. J. Lawlor, A. O'Leary, P. Kavanagh, D. J. O'Brien (capt), J. S. McCarthy.

Referee: I. David (Wales)

Apr 5 1952 – **FRANCE** – Paris – Won 6-3

France: G. Brun, M. Pomathios, J. Mauran, M. Prat, J. Colombier, J. Carabignac, P. Lasaosa, R. Bienes, P. Labadie, R. Brejassou, L. Mias, B. Chevallier, J. Prat, G. Basquet (capt), J. R. Bourdeu.

Scorer: T. Pomathios

England: P. J. Collins, C. E. Winn, A. E. Agar, B. Boobbyer, R. C. Bazley, N. M. Hall (capt), P. W. Sykes, R. V. Stirling, E. Evans, W. A. Holmes, J. R. C. Matthews, D. T. Wilkins, A. O. Lewis, J. MacG. Kendall-Carpenter, D. F. White.

Scorers: P. Hall 2

Referee: W. C. W. Murdoch (Scotland)

Jan 17 1953 – **WALES** – Cardiff – Won 8-3

Wales: T. E. Davies, K. J. Jones, B. L. Williams, M. C. Thomas, G. M. Griffiths, R. Burnett, W. A. Williams, J. D. Robins, G. Beckingham, W. O. Williams, E. R. John, J. R. G. Stephens, S. Judd, J. A. Gwilliam (capt), W. D. Johnson.

Scorer: P. Davies

England: N. M. Hall (capt), J. E. Woodward, A. E. Agar, L. B. Cannell, R. C. Bazley, M. Regan, P. W. Sykes, R. V. Stirling, N. A. Labuschagne, W. A. Holmes, S. J. Adkins, D. T. Wilkins, A. O. Lewis, J. MacG. Kendall-Carpenter, D. F. White.
Scorers: T. Cannell, C. Hall, P. Woodward
Referee: M. J. Dowling (Ireland)

Feb 14 1953 – **IRELAND** – Dublin – Drawn 9-9
Ireland: R. J. Gregg, M. F. Lane, N. J. Henderson, K. Quinn, M. Mortell, J. W. Kyle (capt), J. A. O'Meara, F. E. Anderson, R. J. Roe, W. A. O'Neill, J. R. Brady, T. E. Reid, J. R. Kavanagh, W. E. Bell, J. S. McCarthy.
Scorers: T. Mortell, P. Henderson 2
England: N. M. Hall (capt), J. E. Woodward, A. E. Agar, L. B. Cannell, R. C. Bazley, M. Regan, P. W. Sykes, R. V. Stirling, E. Evans, W. A. Holmes, S. J. Adkins, D. T. Wilkins, A. O. Lewis, J. MacG. Kendall-Carpenter, D. F. White.
Scorers: T. Evans, P. Hall 2
Referee: A. W. C. Austin (Scotland)

Feb 28 1953 – **FRANCE** – Twickenham – Won 11-0
England: N. M. Hall (capt), J. E. Woodward, J. J. Butterfield, L. B. Cannell, R. C. Bazley, M. Regan, P. W. Sykes, R. V. Stirling, E. Evans, W. A. Holmes, S. J. Adkins, D. T. Wilkins, A. O. Lewis, J. MacG. Kendall-Carpenter, D. S. Wilson.
Scorers: T. Butterfield, Evans, Woodward, C. Hall
France: G. Brun, J. R. Bourdeu, M. Prat, J. Mauran, L. Roge, A. Haget, G. Dufau, R. Carrere, J. Arrieta, P. Bertrand, R. Brejassou, B. Chevallier, R. Bienes, M. Celeya, J. Prat (capt).
Referee: V. J. Parfitt (Wales)

Mar 21 1953 – **SCOTLAND** – Twickenham – Won 26-8
England: N. M. Hall (capt), J. E. Woodward, J. J. Butterfield, W. P. C. Davies, R. C. Bazley, M. Regan, D. W. Shuttleworth, R. V. Stirling, E. Evans, W. A. Holmes, S. J. Adkins, D. T. Wilkins, A. O. Lewis, J. MacG. Kendall-Carpenter, D. F. White.
Scorers: T. Bazley 2, Adkins, Butterfield, Stirling, Woodward, C. Hall 4
Scotland: I. H. M. Thomson, J. S. Swan, A. Cameron (capt), D. Cameron, T. G. Weatherstone, L. Bruce-Lockhart, A. F. Dorward, J. C. Dawson, J. H. F. King, R. L. Wilson, J. H. Henderson, J. J. Hegarty, W. Kerr, W. L. K. Cowie, K. H. D. McMillan.
Scorers: T. Henderson, Weatherstone, C. Thomson
Referee: M. J. Dowling (Ireland)

Jan 16 1954 – **WALES** – Twickenham – Won 9-6
England: I. King, J. E. Woodward, J. J. Butterfield, J. P. Quinn, C. E. Winn, M. Regan, G. Rimmer, R. V. Stirling (capt), E. Evans, D. L. Sanders, P. D. Young, P. G. Yarranton, D. S. Wilson, J. MacG. Kendall-Carpenter, R. Higgins.
Scorers: T. Woodward 2, Winn

Wales: G. Williams, K. J. Jones, A. G. Thomas, G. John, G. Rowlands, C. I. Morgan, W. R. Willis, C. C. Meredith, D. M. Davies, W. O. Williams, E. R. John, J. A. Gwilliam, S. Judd, J. R. G. Stephens, R. C. C. Thomas.
Scorers: T. Rowlands, P. Rowlands
Referee: M. J. Dowling (Ireland)

Jan 30 1954 – **NEW ZEALAND** – Twickenham – Lost 0-5
England: I. King, J. E. Woodward, J. J. Butterfield, J. P. Quinn, W. P. C. Davies, M. Regan, G. Rimmer, R. V. Stirling (capt), E. Evans, D. L. Sanders, P. D. Young, P. G. Yarranton, D. S. Wilson, J. MacG. Kendall-Carpenter, R. Higgins.
New Zealand: R. W. H. Scott, M. J. Dixon, C. J. Loader, D. D. Wilson, R. A. Jarden, L. S. Haig, K. Davis, K. L. Skinner, R. C. Hemi, H. L. White, R. A. White, G. N. Dalzell, P. F. H. Jones, R. C. Stuart (capt), W. H. Clark.
Scorers: T. Dalzell, C. Scott
Referee: I. David (Wales)

Feb 13 1954 – **IRELAND** – Twickenham – Won 14-3
England: I. King, J. E. Woodward, J. J. Butterfield, J. P. Quinn, W. P. C. Davies, M. Regan, G. Rimmer, R. V. Stirling (capt), E. Evans, D. L. Sanders, P. D. Young, P. G. Yarranton, D. S. Wilson, J. MacG. Kendall-Carpenter, R. Higgins.
Scorers: T. Butterfield, Regan, Wilson, C. King, P. King
Ireland: R. J. Gregg, M. Mortell, N. J. Henderson, A. C. Pedlow, J. T. Gaston, W. J. Hewitt, J. A. O'Meara, F. E. Anderson, R. J. Roe, B. G. M. Wood, P. J. Lawlor, R. H. Thompson, G. F. Reidy, J. Murphy-O'Connor, J. S. McCarthy (capt).
Scorer: P. Murphy-O'Connor
Referee: A. I. Dickie (Scotland)

Apr 10 1954 – **FRANCE** – Paris – Lost 3-11
France: P. Albaladejo, A. Boniface, R. Martine, M. Prat, F. Cazenave, A. Haget, G. Dufau, R. Bienes, P. Labadie, A. Domenech, A. Sanac, M. Celaya, H. Domec, R. Baulon, J. Prat (capt).
Scorers: T. Boniface, M. Prat, C. J. Prat, P. J. Prat
England: N. Gibbs, J. E. Woodward, J. J. Butterfield, J. P. Quinn, C. E. Winn, M. Regan, J. E. Williams, R. V. Stirling (capt), E. Evans, D. L. Sanders, V. H. Leadbetter, P. D. Young, D. S. Wilson, J. MacG. Kendall-Carpenter, A. O. Lewis.
Scorer: Wilson
Referee: I. David (Wales)

OXFORD VARSITY MATCHES

Dec 7 1948 – **CAMBRIDGE UNIVERSITY** – Twickenham – Won 14-8
Oxford U: A. Stewart, D. W. Swarbrick, C. B. van Ryneveld, L. B. Cannell, D. J. W. Bridge, M. B. Hofmeyr, R. Green, C. T. M. Wilson, H. J. Meadows,

J. MacG. Kendall-Carpenter, G. A. Wilson (capt), A. N. Vintcent, A. J. van Ryneveld, P. W. Kininmonth, R. D. Gill.

Scorers: T. Gill, C. B. van Ryneveld 2, C. Stewart, D. G. Hofmeyr

Cambridge U: W. B. Holmes, A. W. Scott, J. V. Smith, H. M. Kimberley, L. G. Gloag, G. Davies, A. F. Dorward, T. S. McRoberts, R. V. Thompson, P. J. de A. Moore, A. M. James, J. A. Gwilliam, H. H. Mills, A. P.de Nobriga, W. G. Jenkins.

Scorers: T. Davies, C. Holmes, P. Holmes

Referee: A. S. Bean (Durham)

Dec 6 1949 – **CAMBRIDGE UNIVERSITY** – Twickenham – Won 3-0

Oxford U: M. B. Hofmeyr, I. J. Botting, B. Boobbyer, L. B. Cannell, P. J. Langley, C. B. van Ryenveld, R. Green, J. MacG. Kendall-Carpenter, W. J. Hefer, D. A. Emms, A. N. Vintcent (capt), G. N. Gent, A. B. Curtis, G. C. Rittson-Thomas, H. D, Small.

Scorer: T. Gent

Cambridge U: J. C. Davies, I. S. Gloag, J. V. Smith, J. M. Williams, B. M. Jones, G. Davies, A. F. Dorward (capt), G. P. Vaughan, R. V. Thompson, H. Willis, A. M. James, J. M. Jenkins, R. C. C. Thomas, P. D. Young, G. A. B. Covell.

Referee: A. S. Bean (Durham)

Dec 5 1950 – **CAMBRIDGE UNIVERSITY** – Twickenham – Won 8-0

Oxford U: D. J. Lewis, I. J. Botting, B. Boobbyer, L. B. Cannell, C. E. Winn, M. B. Hofmeyr, R. Green, C. J. L. Griffith, W. J. Hefer, D. A. Emms, G. L. Bullard, M. Walker, H. D. Small, J. MacG. Kendall-Carpenter (capt), G. C. Rittson-Thomas.

Scorers: T. Emms, C. Hofmeyr, P. Hofmeyr

Cambridge U: M. J. M. Thompson, J. V. Smith, E. W. Marsden, P. B. Reeve, I. S. Gloag, G. Davies (capt), J. K. Shepherd, R. H. King, C. C. U. Williams, H. D. Doherty, H. Willis, N. E. Williams, C. Barrow, T. R. Marshall, G. M. D. Archer.

Referee: T. Jones (Wales)

BARBARIANS MATCHES

Mar 3 1949 – **EAST MIDLANDS** – Bedford – Won 24-11

Barbarians: W. B. Holmes, K. J. Jones, B. L. Williams, L. G. Gloag, T. J. Danby, G. Davies, H. Tanner (capt), T. W. Price, A. P. Henderson, W. M. Jackson, J. A. Gwilliam, J. R. C. Matthews, M. R. Steele-Bodger, J. MacG. Kendall-Carpenter, G. Evans.

Scorers: T. Williams 2, Gwilliam, Jackson, Danby, Jones, C. Holmes 3

Apr 16 1949 – **CARDIFF** – Won 6-5

Cardiff: F. Trott, R. Burn, B. L. Williams (capt), St. J. Rees, T. Cook, W. B. Cleaver, W. R. Willis, C. Davies, J. R. Phillips, G. Jenkins, P. Goodfellow, S. Judd, E. Jones, J. D. Nelson, G. Evans.

Scorers: T. Nelson, C. Judd

Barbarians: W. B. Holmes, W. D. McKee, L. F. L. Oakley, C. B. van Ryneveld, M. F. Lane, J. W. Kyle, H.de Lacy, T. W. Price, J. H. Steeds, D. H. Keller, J. E. Nelson, R. D. Agar, J. MacG. Kendall-Carpenter, B. H. Travers (capt), J. S. McCarthy.
Scorers: T. Lane, Kyle

Apr 19 1949 – **NEWPORT** – Won 6-5
Newport: R. Hughes, R. Wade, A. G. Stephens, C. Gibbons, C. Perrins, R. J. Burnett, H. Thomas, R. Rowland, R. Clarke, E. Coleman, L. E. T. Jones, P. Davies (capt), D. Dando, S. Kimpton, R. T. Evans.
Scorers: T. Burnett, C. Davies
Barbarians: G. W. Norton, B. Mullan, W. B. Holmes, W. D. McKee, J. W. Kyle, P. M. Fletcher, L. Griffin, J. A. R. McPhail, J. MacG. Kendall-Carpenter, J. E. Nelson, R. D. Agar, J. S. McCarthy, B. H. Travers(capt), M. R. Steele-Bodger.
Scorers: P. Holmes, D. G. Holmes

Dec 27 1949 – **LEICESTER** – Won 29-0
Leicester: H. B. Deacon, W. K. Nicholas, G. H. Cullen, D. A. Quine, D. E. P. Rees, J. P. Morris, W. K. T. Moore, P. L. Thorneloe, R. E. Tudor, S. T. H. Wright, D. Norton, R. H. Smith, A. C. Towell (capt), J. R. Day, H. W. Sibson.
Barbarians: M. B. Hofmeyr, I. J. Botting, B. Boobbyer, C. B. van Ryneveld, J. P. Hyde, T. A. Kemp (capt), H. Thomas, T. W. Price, J. H. Steeds, J. MacG. Kendall-Carpenter, A. N. Vintcent, G. R. D'A. Hosking, H. D. Small, P. B. C. Moore, M. R. Steele-Bodger.
Scorers: T. Kemp, Small, Hosking, Moore, Thomas, C. Hofmeyr 4, P. Hofmeyr 2

Mar 2 1950 – **EAST MIDLANDS** – Northampton – Lost 3-5
E. Midlands: H. W. Rose, P. Collindridge, L. F. L. Oakley, L. B. Cannell, N. Bailey, T. A. Gray, F. M. Fletcher, J. H. White, J. H. Keeling, M. J. Berridge, W. R. Hamp, J. F. Bance, G. Jenkins, R. G. Furbank, D. F. White.
Scorers: T. Bailey, C. Gray
Barbarians: G. Williams, C. W. Drummond, B. Boobbyer, R. McDonald, G. H. Sullivan, I. Preece, P. W. Sykes, J. C. Dawson, J. H. Steeds, G. M. Budge, S. J. Adkins, J. R. C. Matthews, P. B. C. Moore, J. MacG. Kendall-Carpenter (capt), H. D. Small.
Scorers: T. Williams

Dec 27 1950 – **LEICESTER** – Drawn 13-13
Leicester: R. Marshall, W. K. Nicholas, G. H. Cullen, H. G. Thomas, C. G. Lawrence, J. P. Morris, W. K. T. Moore (capt), J. H. Hacker, S. Pratt, R. D. Bolesworth, R. V. Stirling, E. Lacey, J. C. Kail, T. H. Bleasdale, H. W. Sibson.
Scorers: T. Lawrence, Thomas, Sibson, C. Morris 2
Barbarians: M. B. Hofmeyr, J. V. Smith, B. Boobbyer, I. Preece, C. E. Winn, E. M. P. Hardy, D. W. Shuttleworth, J. D. Robins, W. J. Hefer, H. Willis, E. R. John, J. F. Bance, H. D. Small, J. MacG. Kendall-Carpenter, W. I. D. Elliot.
Scorers: T. Elliot, Winn, Kendall-Carpenter, C. Hofmeyr 2

Mar 24 1951– CARDIFF – Lost 3-13
Barbarians: G. Williams, M. Pomathios, D. M. Scott, D. M. Rose, F. O. Turnbull, E. M. P. Hardy, D. W. Shuttleworth, T. Clifford, R. J. Roe, D. McKibbin, J. E. Nelson (capt), E. R. John, J. MacG. Kendall-Carpenter, P. W. Kininmonth, H. D. Small.
Scorers: P. McKibbin

Mar 27 1951 – NEWPORT – Lost 6-13
Barbarians: G. Williams, M. Pomathios, J. M. Williams, D. M. Rose, F. O. Turnbull, W. J. Hewitt, H. McCracken, J. C. Dawson, R. J. Roe, D. McKibbin, H. M. Inglis, E. R. John, J. MacG. Kendall-Carpenter, J. R. G. Stephens (capt), R. C. Taylor.
Scorers: T. J. M. Williams 2

Dec 27 1951 – LEICESTER – Lost 8-13
Leicester: J. W. Fisk, W. K. Nicholas, G. H. Cullen, H. G. Thomas, C. G. Lawrence, M. R. Channer, W. K. T. Moore (capt), R. V. Stirling, S. Pratt, R. D. Bolesworth, E. Lacey, R. H. Smith, E. A. Barrow, T. H. Bleasdale, H. W. Sibson.
Scorers: T. Thomas, Smith, Sibson, C. Cullen 2
Barbarians: G. Williams, J. E. Woodward, B. Boobbyer, M. C. Thomas, R. C. Bazeley, C. I. Morgan, W. R. Willis, E. E. Woodgate, D. M. Davies, W. Woodgate, H. A. Jones, J. R. C. Matthews, J. MacG. Kendall-Carpenter, J. A. Gwilliam (capt), G. L. Bullard.
Scorers: T. Boobbyer, Gwilliam, C. Thomas

Jan 26 1952 – SOUTH AFRICA – Cardiff – Lost 3-17
Barbarians: G. Williams, J. E. Woodward, B. L. Williams, L. B. Cannell, K. J. Jones, C. I. Morgan, W. R. Willis, R. V. Stirling, D. M. Davies, J. MacG. Kendall-Carpenter, E. R. John, J. E. Nelson (capt), W. I. D. Elliot, J. R. G. Stephens, V. G. Roberts.
Scorer: T. Elliot
South Africa: A. C. Keevy, F. P. Marais, R. A. M. van Schoor, M. T. Lategan, J. K. Ochse, P. G. Johnstone, P. A. du Toit, F. E. van der Ryst, W. Delport, H. J. Bekker, J. M. du Rand, E. Dinkelmann, S. P. Fry, H. S. V. Muller, C. J. van Wyk.
Scorers: T. Ochse van Wyk, C. Keevy, P. Keevy 2, Johnstone
Referee: M. J. Dowling

Dec 26 1952 – LEICESTER – Won 22-9
Leicester: R. Marshall, I. J. Botting, G. H. Cullen, G. Randle, C. G. Lawrence, M. R. Channer, W. K. T. Moore, P. L. Thorneloe, S. Pratt, R. D. Bolesworth (capt), R. H. Smith, R. V. Stirling, P. H. Konig, J. M. Jenkins, A. E. Barrow.
Scorers: T. Lawrence, P. Channer, D. G. Channer
Barbarians: I. King, B. M. Gray, J. J. Butterfield, L. B. Cannell, D. A. Barker, N. Davidson, A. F. Dorward (capt), D. A. Emms, D. M. Davies, W. A. Holmes, J. T. Bartlett, D. T. Wilkins, D. S. Wilson, J. MacG. Kendall-Carpenter, D. F. White.
Scorers: T. Cannell, Butterfield, White, Barker, C. King 2, P. King 2

Mar 5 1953 – **EAST MIDLANDS** – Bedford – Lost 5-8
Barbarians: I. King, W. P. C. Davies, J. J. Butterfield, A. G. Thomas, H. Morris,
J. W. Kyle (capt), K. M. Spence, F. E. Anderson, R. J. Roe, W. A. O'Neill,
S. J. Adkins, D. T. Wilkins, A. O. Lewis, J. MacG. Kendall-Carpenter,
D. S. Wilson.
Scorers: T. Lewis, C. King

Apr 3 1953 – **PENARTH** – Won 13-3
Barbarians: C. J. Saunders, J. A. Gregory, B. L. Williams (capt), D. M. Greenwood,
T. G. Weatherstone, D. G. S. Baker, J. A. O'Meara, J. D. Robins, F. R. Beringer,
E. E. Woodgate, P. J. F. Wheeler, J. F. Bance, J. R. G. Stephens, J. MacG. Kendall-
Carpenter, N. G. Davies.
Scorers: T. Woodgate 2, C. Robins 2, P. Robins

Apr 6 1953 – **SWANSEA** – Won 18-8
Barbarians: I. A. King (capt), B. M. Gray, D. M. Greenwood, G. M. Griffiths,
T. G. Weatherstone, D. G. S. Baker, J. A. O'Meara, W. A. O'Neill, E. Robinson,
E. E. Woodgate, E. R. John, J. R. G. Stephens, W. E. Bell, J. MacG. Kendall-
Carpenter, R. C. C. Thomas.
Scorers: T. Griffiths 3, Gray, C. King 3

Dec 28 1954 – **LEICESTER** – Won 22-13
Leicester: R. Marshall, J. E. Taylor, J. J. Elders, D. Brook, G. H. Cullen,
M. R. Channer, T. O'Connor, F. Chawner, J. Stevens, D. St. G. Hazell,
E. C. Lacey, R. H. Smith, T. H. Bleasdale, J. M. Jenkins (capt),
P. H. Konig.
Scorers: T. Elders, Channer, C. Hazell 2, P. Hazell
Barbarians: N. S. D. Estcourt, F. D. Sykes, J. J. Butterfield, P. G. Johnstone,
B. M. Gray, J. T. Docherty, D. W. Shuttleworth, F. E. Anderson, E. Evans (capt),
D. R. McKibbin, P. J. Taylor, R. H. Thompson, P. H. Ryan, J. MacG. Kendall-
Carpenter, R. Higgins.
Scorers: T. Ryan, Sykes, Thompson, Gray, Higgins, C. Johnstone 2, P. McKibbin

COMBINED COUNTIES MATCHES

Oct 13 1951 – **SOUTH AFRICA** – Plymouth – Lost 8-17
S. W. Counties: P. J. Collins, B. M. Gray, J. M. Williams, P. M. Luffman,
R. M. Holgate, H. Oliver, M. G. Andrews, E. E. Woodgate, F. Sampson,
W. Woodgate, G. F. Stride, H. A. Jones (capt), A. Bone, J. MacG. Kendall-
Carpenter, V. G. Roberts.
Scorers: T. W. Woodgate, C. Oliver, P. Oliver
South Africa: A. C. Keevy, F. P. Marais, S. S. Viviers, M. T. Lategan, J. K. Ochse,
D. Fry, J. Oelofse, A. Geffin, P. Wessels, F. van der Ryst, G. Dannhauser,
J. Pickard, S. P. Fry, H. S. V. Muller (capt), B. Myburgh.
Scorers: T. Myburgh, C. Geffin, P. Geffin 4
Referee: T. N. Pearce

Dec 9 1953 – **NEW ZEALAND** – Camborne – Lost 0-9

S. W. Counties: C. T. Bowen, H. Stevens, J. M. Williams, C. M. Terry, J. L. Stark, H. Oliver, R. F. G. Meadows, E. E. Woodgate, B. V. Meredith, W. Woodgate, I. Zaidman, T. K. Vivian, A. Bone, J. MacG. Kendall-Carpenter (capt), V. G. Roberts.

New Zealand: J. W. Kelly, M. J. Dixon, J. M. Tanner, C. J. Loader, R. A. Jarden, L. S. Haig (capt), K. Davis, H. L. White, C. A. Woods, K. L. Skinner, K. P. Bagley, G. N. Dalzell, P. F. Jones, I. J. Clarke, W. H. Clark.

Scorers: T. Davis, P. Jarden, D. G. Haig

Referee: H. B. Elliott (Durham)

COUNTY SEMI-FINAL

Feb 5 1955   **MIDDLESEX**   Redruth   Lost 3-10

Cornwall: H.Stevens   G.G.Luke   J.M.Williams   R.W.Hosen   R.F.P.Carne J.Morgan   T.Thomas   T.Bidgood   A.L.Semmens   P.D.Cleaver   C.R.Johns G.Harris   A.Bone   J.MacG.Kendall-Carpenter (capt)   V.G.Roberts.

Scorer: P Stevens

Middlesex: N.M.Hall   J.E.Woodward   P.C.Delight   J.G.Palmer   P.H.Ryan D.G.S.Baker   J.E.Williams   J.F.Herbert   N.Labuschagne   J.H.Smith P.G.Yarranton   V.J.S.Harding   D.S.Gilbert-Smith   J.S.Ritchie   R.E.Syrett.

Scorers: T Gilbert-Smith Baker C Hall 2

Referee: Dr.B.S.Mills (Northumberland)